The Art of Engaging Unionised Employees

Jan Hendrick Nel • Bennie Linde

The Art of Engaging Unionised Employees

palgrave
macmillan

Jan Hendrick Nel
People and Business Solutions
BDO South Africa
Johannesburg, South Africa

Bennie Linde
Economic and Management Faculty
North-West University
Potchefstroom, South Africa

ISBN 978-981-13-2196-2 ISBN 978-981-13-2197-9 (eBook)
https://doi.org/10.1007/978-981-13-2197-9

Library of Congress Control Number: 2018953989

This Palgrave Pivot imprint is published by the registered company Springer Nature Singapore Pte Ltd.
The registered company address is: 152 Beach Road, #21-01/04 Gateway East, Singapore 189721, Singapore

Contents

About the Authors

Jan Hendrick Nel is the HR director for BDO South Africa and the head of BDO People and Business Solutions. Nel holds a master's degree in Human Resource Management and Industrial Relations and is currently working on his PhD. He has many years of international experience, representing BDO Sub Sahara Africa on the BDO International HR and Development Committee. Nel is a member of the South African Board of Professional Practitioners as a Master Practitioner.

Bennie Linde is an associate professor at the North-West University in South Africa. He is a member of the Faculty of Economic and Management Sciences of the School of Industrial Psychology and Human Resource Management where he teaches under- and postgraduate modules in employment relations management and supervises masters and PhD students. Linde is the chairperson of the Economic and Management Sciences Research Ethics Committee of the North-West University. He has been an active employment relations practitioner for more than two decades.

Acronyms

ASTD	The American Society for Training and Development
CIMO	Context, Interventions, Mechanisms and Outcomes
EOR	Employee-Organisation Relationship
HPWO	High-Performance Work Organisations and Environments
HRM	Human Resource Management
JD-R	Job Demands-Resource Model
LME	Leader Member Exchange
OCB	Organisational Citizenship Behaviours
ROA	Return on Assets
SET	Social Exchange Theory
SHRM	Society for Human Resources
UWES	Utrecht Work Engagement Scale

List of Figures

List of Tables

CHAPTER 1

Introduction

Abstract This chapter is an overview of the systematic review and narrative evidence synthesis from the literature on engagement to develop a new framework to increase the low levels of engagement in a unionised environment. Although much has been written on engagement, no research has been done to understand employee engagement in a unionised environment. Various propositions emerged from the systematic review and the evidence synthesis of the literature to create a conceptual framework on how to increase the engagement levels in a unionised environment. Findings show that employee engagement can be fostered in organisations with a unionised presence by focusing on job design factors, trust and integrity, individual characteristics, collaborative partnerships, employee voice, human resources management practices and leadership and line managers' behaviour as antecedents to engagement.

Keywords Conceptual framework • Employee engagement • Narrative evidence synthesis • Systematic review

Organisations are increasingly challenged to develop strategies to manage their human resources in difficult times, and one of the strategies proposed is embracing employee engagement (CIPD 2012). Employee engagement has become one of the most popular topics in management and the past decade has seen an explosion of research and heightened interest in the

J. H. Nel, B. Linde, *The Art of Engaging Unionised Employees*,
https://doi.org/10.1007/978-981-13-2197-9_1

concept (Saks and Gruman 2014). Employee engagement proposes a reciprocal employment relationship between employers and employees, creating a mutually beneficial relationship that is a key factor for an organisation's success, sustained competitive advantage and profitability (Saks and Gruman 2014).

The meaning of engagement might be easy to recognise in practice, but difficult to define and no widely accepted definition of engagement is currently in use (Saks and Gruman 2014; Schaufeli 2013). Engagement has been plagued by disagreement about its nature, since it was conceptualised by Kahn (1990), due to its overlap with other traditional concepts (Schaufeli 2013). The most evident overlap is with job-related attitudes, job behaviour and behavioural intentions, health and well-being, and personality traits (Schaufeli 2013).

Whittington et al. (2017) mention that researchers have described engagement as the conditions that lead to engagement, while others suggest that engagement is a personality trait and some view engagement as a state of motivation. The state approach to engagement, according to Whittington et al. (2017), reflects Kahn's (1990) conceptualisation of engagement as "the harnessing of organisation members' selves to their work roles: in engagement, people employ and express themselves physically, cognitively, emotionally and mentally during role performance" (p. 694).

Kahn's (1990) conceptual work was the first to provide a foundation for the theoretical development of employee engagement. His further quests for understanding of the self-in-role process and the roles people occupy at work led to Kahn (1990) creating the term "engagement". Kahn (1990) defined personal engagement as "the harnessing of organisation members' selves to their work roles: in engagement, people employ and express themselves physically, cognitively, emotionally and mentally during role performance" (Kahn 1990, p. 694).

It seems that organisations believe that by managing a range of variables, known as antecedents of engagement, they can effectively manage the consequences of engagement and increase the engagement levels of its employees (Saks and Gruman 2014). Crawford et al. (2014) are of the opinion that the majority of the antecedents reflects the three psychological conditions identified by Kahn (1990) in his foundational theory, namely meaningfulness, safety and availability. The theme underlying Kahn's (1990) research is that the individuals' perception of the organisation, job and personal characteristics affects the experience of the three psychological conditions, which in turn guide the individuals' decisions to engage more completely in their work roles (Crawford et al. 2014).

The consequences of high engagement levels are promoted to be what most organisations are pursuing (Bailey et al. 2015). High levels of engagement can lead to enhanced employee performance, and in turn higher profitability, revenue generation and organisational growth (Christian et al. 2011; Rich et al. 2010; Macey and Schneider 2008; Holbeche and Springett 2003; Harter et al. 2002; Wollard and Shuck 2011). Engagement and employee retention have emerged as a leading concern for organisations and those that actively enhance employee engagement will accomplish something that their competitors will find difficult to replicate (Kumar and Swetha 2011). Employee engagement has the potential to enhance both individual well-being and organisational performance, circumventing the traditional trade-offs and tension that exists between employer and employees within the human resource and industrial relations domains (Truss et al. 2013).

Although engagement has become increasingly mainstream in management over the past decade, it has been reported that engagement is on the decline worldwide and that there is a deepening disengagement among employees (Saks 2006). According to Gallup (2014), as cited in Bersin (2015), disengagement is a worldwide trend and that only 13% of employees were "highly" engaged and that 26% were "actively" disengaged. This trend validates concerns about the levels of disengagement, as disengaged employees display counterproductive workplace behaviour that impacts negatively on business outcomes (Whittington et al. 2017).

Research of Donais (2010) and Tyler (2009) suggests that unionised employees are less engaged than their non-union counterparts are. According to Crabtree (2006), a study that was published in the Gallup Management Journal shows that 26% of union employees and 35% of non-union employees engaged, that 50% of union employees and 50% of union employees are disengaged and that 23% of union employees and 15% on non-union employees are actively disengaged. Gallup, according to Crabtreee (2006, p. 3), defines engaged employees as "employees who work with a passion and feel a profound connection to their company, that they drive innovation and move the organisation forward". Disengaged employees, on the other hand, are essentially "checked out, they sleepwalk through their workday, putting time, but not energy or passion into their work". Actively disengaged employees aren't just unhappy at work; they are busy acting out their unhappiness. Every day, these workers undermine what their engaged co-workers accomplish.

Employees often join unions in an attempt to increase satisfaction, but never achieve the same satisfaction levels as their non-unionised peers (Sheridan and Anderson 2013). Guest and Conway (2002) postulate that their dissatisfaction may have something to do with being a union member. While workers join trade unions to benefit from their collective membership, there are very limited returns by way of specific outcomes or greater voice (Guest and Conway 2002). According to Donais (2010), the reason for the higher disengagement levels amongst unionised employees is the relationship the union has with its employer. The impact of disengagement in companies with a union presence is often more significant, since union members' dissatisfaction can spread to their co-workers and lead to overall negative sentiments towards the organisation as a whole (Sheridan and Anderson 2013). Furthermore, union members are more likely to remain with one organisation throughout their careers and their dissatisfaction will impact on the engagement levels of the entire workforce and have an adverse impact on any engagement efforts (Sheridan and Anderson 2013).

Research on engagement has exclusively focused on non-union employees, which is questionable, because there is an increasing understanding that the development of employee potential cannot exclusively be focused on non-union employees (Donais 2010). Understanding engagement in a unionised environment is just as important as engagement in a non-unionised environment, due to the correlation between engagement and positive individual and organisational outcomes (Sheridan and Anderson 2013).

The differences between unionised and non-unionised employees, however, make engaging unionised employees more challenging (Donais 2010). Employers see the value of engaging all employees, but fail to successfully implement engagement strategies in unionised environments, leading to resentment as they realise that unions can directly influence the outcomes of engagement efforts (Donais 2010).

The problem is that unionised employees are less engaged than non-unionised employees, and although a wide range of frameworks have been developed to explain engagement, no framework has been developed to explain how engagement levels of unionised employees can be increased. The purpose of this book is to develop an engagement framework that will address the low levels of engagement in a unionised environment.

The claim that unionised employees are less engaged than non-unionised employees has not previously been tested through a systematic review. We will present the findings of a narrative evidence synthesis that focusses on the following five questions:

1. How has engagement been defined and conceptualised within academic and practitioner literature?
2. What do academics and practitioners recognise as conditions for high levels of engagement?
3. What reported circumstances influence engagement levels in a unionised environment?
4. What approaches and interventions have the greatest potential to create and embed high levels of engagement in a unionised environment?
5. What could a framework for engagement in a unionised environment look like in order to increase engagement levels?

The identification of relevant literature streams was based on these five questions.

Kahn's (1990, 1992) model of engagement and disengagement was adopted and extended on to create a framework to employee engagement in a unionised environment. Following Kahn's (1990, 1992) and Rich et al.'s (2010) conceptualisation of engagement, the framework will view engagement as the investment of an individual's complete self, physically, cognitively and emotionally during role performance.

Literature Review Method

To address these issues a systematic review and narrative synthesis of the evidence on employee engagement literature was conducted.

This narrative evidence synthesis adopted the guidelines establish by Briner and Denyer (2012) to determine the quality, relevance, transparency, replicability and credibility of research. We followed the five steps outlined by Briner and Denyer (2012), namely planning, structured search, evaluating material against agreed eligibility criteria, analysis and thematic coding, and reporting.

The search strategy adopted a dual approach. As the focus of the review was academic in nature, the review of literature was primarily focused only on academic works, including seminal publications, frameworks and models that informed the academic conceptualisation of employee engagement; and the second focused on a review of practitioners' literature. The data was collected through a structured search of literature on engagement using an exact phrase search approach across a number of databases and different disciplines in the field of psychology, business management, economics, sociology, philosophy and industrial relations. The search was confined to literature which was published after 1990, when Kahn (1990) published his seminal work on engagement. The search strategy was further improved by citation tracking, scanning reference lists, endnotes and footnotes for additional material not identified by the databases.

The structured search yielded 382 sources form the various fields which were extracted and considered for data analysis using the context, interventions, mechanisms and outcomes (CIMO) method to map the issues, focus the question and test their logic (Denyer and Transfield 2009).

Using the CIMO framework led to the exclusion of 194 records, because it did not meet the inclusion criteria. The net result was that only 188 literature sources were eligible for further assessment. The 188 sources were critically evaluated against inclusion criteria and data was extracted from the included material as the basis of the synthesis. A further 58 sources were excluded because they did not meet the inclusion criteria. Complete versions of the 130 sources were shortlisted in order to evaluate and data extract from them.

The purpose of including practitioner's literature review was to include any relevant materials in this evidence synthesis to enhance rigour and, specifically to address question five, to consider what materials and tools from this wider resource might be of relevance to practitioners in the unionised context. In the end, only 13 sources of relevant, good-quality evidence were identified, from which 14 items describing various tools and resources were obtained. Analysis of these materials identified a number of important themes linked to engagement, including meaningfulness, leadership, line manager's behaviour, performance reviews, trust and employee voice. Although there were broad similarities between the overall themes in the academic and the practitioners' literature concerning engagement, the review of the practitioners' material focuses more on wider managerial and human resources issues rather than on the psychological factors of engagement.

The shortlisted sources were organised according to their specific relevance to the questions. After the systematic review of all the studies relating to the review questions, a narrative synthesis of the evidence was performed to synthesise the evidence as proposed by (Briner and Denyer 2012). The topic of engagement has reached a sufficient stage of maturity to warrant a narrative review in order to synthesise the current evidence-base and provide a foundation for advancing the knowledge in engagement in a unionised environment.

The purpose of this was to identify emerging themes from the literature to narrate the findings from the various studies together to develop new insights into engagement in general, and within the context of a unionised environment. The approach to synthesising the data mirrors that suggested by Popay et al. (2006, pp. 11–16), who argued that a narrative synthesis should seek to explore the relationships in the extracted data within and between studies. Emerging themes in the data were identified and clustered together.

A synthesis of the emerging themes was done by analysing the relationship between data and its contents and a framework was constructed from the new themes. The evidence was presented in the final framework, which provides a comprehensive, logically derived conceptual framework of the antecedents and consequences of engagement in a unionised environment that can be used in empirical studies on this topic.

The robustness of the study was ensured by the amount of studies that was included and the quality of the studies. The application of quality and relevance criteria led to the inclusion of 70 empirical journal articles, 7 research papers and 3 dissertations and 38 books published by leaders in their field in the final data extraction exercise.

The flow of information through the stages of the evidence synthesis is depicted in Fig. 1.1, the PRISMA-style flow chart of reporting the inclusion and exclusion of sources. The flow diagram depicts the flow of information through the different phases of a systematic review. It maps out the number of records identified, included and excluded.

In Chap. 2 an overview of the employee engagement concept is provided. We explore the origins of engagement that led to the existing conceptualisation of engagement in the literature. The current conceptualisation of engagement develops a better understanding of the engagement construct to adopt the most appropriate framework to increase the engagement levels of employees in a unionised environment. Various researched and validated antecedents and outcomes associated with high levels of engagement are identified in Chap. 3. Analysing the

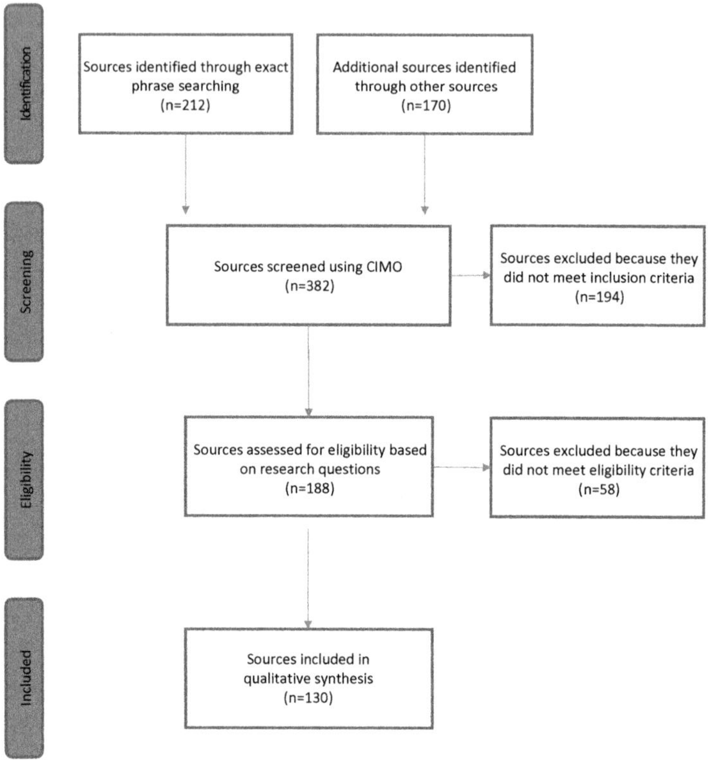

Fig. 1.1 PRISMA-style flow of information through stages 1–4 of the evidence synthesis

data on the antecedents and outcomes enabled us to identify additional antecedents which have the greatest potential to increase the engagement levels in a unionised environment. Engaging unionised employees requires a different approach due to the nature of the employment relationship and the environmental context in which the relationship takes place; this is discussed in Chap. 4. In Chap. 5 we identify the possible reasons for union member dissatisfaction and identify factors associated with healthier union and employer relationships. Chapter 6 provides the findings of the narrative synthesis focusing on 11 propositions to develop the conceptual engagement framework. The framework explains how the individual and organisational antecedent factors can be linked to engagement, which in turn leads to positive individual and organisational outcomes. Our review of the literature is concluded in Chap. 7 with a discussion on the findings of our narrative evidence synthesis and our contribution to the development of the theory on engagement.

References

Bailey, C., Madden, A., Alfes, K., & Fletcher, L. (2015). The meaning, antecedents and outcomes of employee engagement: A narrative synthesis. International Journal of Management Reviews, 00, 1–23. doi:https://doi.org/10.1111/ijmr.12077

Bersin, J. (2015). Becoming irresistible: A new model for employee engagement. Deloitte.

Briner, R., & Denyer, D. (2012). Systematic review and evidence synthesis as a practice and scholarship tool. In D. Rousseau (Ed.), The Oxford Handbook of Evidence-Based Management (pp. 112–119). Oxford: Oxford University Press.

Christian, M. S., Garza, A. S., & Slaughter, J. E. (2011). Work engagement: A qualitative review and test of its relations with task and contextual performance. Personnel Psychology, 64, 89–136.

CIPD. (2012). Managing employee relations in difficult times. London: Chartered Institute of Personnel and Development.

Crabtree, S. (2006, May). Can Managers Engage Unionized Employees? The Gallup Management Journal. Retrieved from http://www.gmj.gallup.com

Crawford, E. R., Rich, B. L., Buckman, B., & Bergeron, J. (2014). The antecedents and drivers of employee engagement. In C. Truss, R. Delbridge, K. Alfes, A. Shantz, & E. Soane, Employee engagement in theory and practice (pp. 57–81). New York: Routledge.

Denyer, D., & Transfield, D. (2009). Producing a systematic review (D. Buchanan, & A. Bryman, Eds.). London: Sage.

Donais, Blaine. (2010). Engaging unionised employees: Employee morale and productivity. Ontario, Canada: Thomson Reuters.

Guest, D. E., & Conway, N. (2002). Pressure at work and the psychological contract. London: CIPD.

Harter, J. K., Schmidt, F. L., & Hayes, T. L. (2002). Business-unit-level relationship between employee satisfaction, employee engagement, and business outcomes: A meta-analysis. Journal of Applied Psychology, 87(2), 268–279.

Holbeche, L., & Springett, N. (2003). In Search of Meaning in the Workplace. Horsham: Roffey Park.

Kahn, W. A. (1990). Psychological conditions of personal engagement and disengagement at work. Academy of Management Journal, 33(4), 692–724.

Kahn, W. A. (1992). To Be Fully There: Psychological Presence at Work. Human Relations 45(4), 321–349.

Kumar, P., & Swetha, G. (2011). A prognostic examination of employee engagement from its historical roots. International Journal of Trade, Economics and Finance, 2(3), 232.

Macey, W., & Schneider, B. (2008). The Meaning of Employee Engagement. Industrial and Organizational Psychology, 3–30.

Popay, J., Roberts, H., Sowden, A., Petticrew, M., Arai, L., Rodgers, M., … Duffy, S. (2006). Guidance on the Conduct of Narrative Synthesis in Systematic Reviews: Final Report. Swindon: ESRC Research Methods Programme.

Rich, B. L., Lepine, J. A., & Crawford, E. R. (2010). Job engagement: Antecedents and effects on job performance. Academy of Management Journal, 53(3), 614–635.

Saks, A. M. (2006). Antecedents and consequences of employee engagement. Journal of Managerial Psychology, 21(7), 600–619.

Saks, A. M., & Gruman, J. A. (2014). What do we really know about employee engagement. Human Resources Development Quarterly, 25(2), 155–182.

Schaufeli, W. (2013). Employee Engagement in Theory and Practice (C. Truss, K. Alfes, R. Delbridge, A. Shantz, & E. Soane, Eds.). London: Routledge.

Sheridan, K., & Anderson, K. (2013, July 24). HR Solutions eNews. Retrieved July 24, 2013, from http://avatarsolutions.com/resources/enews-0311/Unionized-0311.html

Truss, C., Shantz, A., Soane, E., Alfes, K., & Delbridge, R. (2013). Employee engagement, organisational performance and individual well-being: Exploring the evidence, developing the theory. The International Journal of Human Resources Management, 24(14), 2657–2669.

Tyler, J. (2009). Employee Engagement and Labour Relations. Retrieved May 31, 2013, from businessjournal.gallup.com: http://businessjournal.gallup.com

Whittington, J., Meskelis, S., Asare, E., & Beldona, S. (2017). Enhancing Employee Engagement: An Evidence-Based Approach. Cham, Switzerland: Palgrave Macmillan.

Wollard, K. K., & Shuck, B. (2011). Antecedents to Employee Engagement: A structured review of the literature. Advances in Developing Human Resources, 13(4), 429–446.

CHAPTER 2

The Emergence of the Employee Engagement Concept

Abstract This chapter explores the development of engagement through a historical lens using a systematic review of the literature to gain a better understanding of the concepts and frameworks on engagement to develop a foundation for a new framework to address the low levels of engagement in a unionised environment. Literature indicates that there are several definitions of employee engagement in existence and yet there is a lack of consensus regarding the meaning and distinctiveness of employee engagement from other constructs (Saks and Gruman, Hum Resour Dev Q 25(2): 155–182, 2014). Just as there are several definitions of employee engagement, several theories of engagement exist. There are four major theoretical approaches to define the existing state of engagement, namely the need-satisfying approach, the burnout-antithesis approach, the satisfaction-engagement approach, and the multidimensional approach (Shuck, Hum Resour Dev Rev 10(3): 304–328, 2011).

Keywords Conceptualisation of engagement • Definitions of employee engagement • Low levels of engagement • Theoretical approaches • Unionised environment

The purpose to this chapter is to explore the origins and development of engagement, which led to the existing perspective of engagement to

J. H. Nel, B. Linde, *The Art of Engaging Unionised Employees*,
https://doi.org/10.1007/978-981-13-2197-9_2

develop a better understanding of the concepts and frameworks that might inform the most appropriate framework to increase engagement levels in a unionised environment.

Employee engagement has become one of the most popular topics in management and academia, because there is a strong body of research that indicates that engagement is a key factor for an organisation's success, sustained competitive advantage and profitability (Saks and Gruman 2014).

This trend is consistent with claims that there is a general decrease in the overall levels of employee engagement (Bersin 2015). In addition to the overall low levels of engagement observed, engagement levels of unionised employees are even lower than those of their non-unionised counterparts (Crabtree 2006). Concerns about the level of employee engagement are well founded, as it is estimated that the financial costs of disengagement are globally on the increase (Whittington et al. 2017). Not only does disengagement have negative financial implications, but disengaged employees often engage in counterproductive workplace behaviour (Whittington et al. 2017). To sustain business success and counteract low levels of engagement, organisations are shifting their focus from materialistic capital to intellectual capital and employee engagement is viewed as one of the vehicles to achieve this shift (Bhuvanaiah and Raya 2014).

Schaufeli (2013) is of the view that the changes in the nature of work during the past four decades, and a renewed interest in the psychological contract, have created the background for the emergence of engagement in business. The major changes that took place in the world of work were due to the ongoing transition from traditional to modern organisations. This transition forced organisations to review, not only their business models, but also the capabilities of the people they employ. This left unionised employees vulnerable as unions struggle to respond to these changes.

Schaufeli (2013) mentioned that David Ulrich stated that human capital becomes increasingly important, since fewer people are required to do more. Organisations also require employees who are willing to invest in their jobs psychologically. These changes resulted in the "psychologisation of the workplace", which requires a substantial psychological adaption and involvement from employees (Schaufeli 2013, p. 16). Schaufeli (2013, p. 16) elaborated that employees need "...psychological capabilities as modern organisations need employees that are able and willing to invest in their work psychologically". Engagement has been proposed as the vehicle to achieve this.

The History of Employee Engagement

The first mention of employee engagement to appear in management literature was a 1990 *Academy of Management Journal* article, "Psychological Conditions of Personal Engagement and Disengagement at Work" (Kahn 1990). Kahn's (1990) conceptual work was the first to provide a foundation for the theoretical development of employee engagement. Although much of today's research refers to Kahn's work as the theoretical underpinning of employee engagement, it took another decade before the theoretical ideas received significant support from other academics (Welbourne and Schlachter 2014). Schaufeli (2013) suggests that the reason for the delay is due to the gradual changes in the world of work and the emergence of the positive psychology movement that has gained significate momentum since the 1990s.

Conceptually, Kahn began with the work of Goffman (1959), *The Presentation of Self in Everyday Life,* who suggested that people's attachment and detachment to their role varies depending on a person's interactions during brief, face-to-face encounters. This attachment and detachment was the starting point for Kahn's (1990) work towards defining the self-in-role of people. Although Kahn (1990) agreed with Goffman (1959), he suggested that a new perspective was needed to understand engagement in an organisational context. Kahn (1990, p. 694) believed that "employees act out momentary attachment and detachment in role performance at work", a direct reference to Goffman's (1959) interactionist theory, but specific to the workplace (Shuck and Wollard 2009).

To gain further understanding of the varying levels of attachment individuals expressed towards their roles, Kahn (1990) examined several disciplines and found that individuals feel hesitant to belong to an ongoing group or system and thereby naturally tend to pull away from and move towards its membership. As a result, individuals seek to protect themselves from both isolation and engulfment by alternatively pulling away from and moving towards their membership. Kahn (1990) stated that the attachment and detachment of people are people's calibration of self-in-role. Kahn (1990) termed these calibrations of self-in-role as "personal engagement" and "personal disengagement". This means behaviour by which people bring in or leave out their personal selves during work role performance. Kahn's (1990) quest of understanding of the self-in-role process and the roles people occupy at work led to Kahn (1990) creating the term "engagement".

Kahn (1990) undertook a qualitative study on the psychological conditions of personal engagement and disengagement and postulated that there were three psychological conditions related to engagement and disengagement at work. These psychological conditions are meaningfulness, safety and availability. Kahn (1990) found that people are more engaged at work in situations that offered them more psychological meaningfulness and psychological safety, and when they were more psychologically available. According to Rich et al. (2010), Kahn's (1990) definition of engagement is a multidimensional motivational construct that involves the simultaneous investment of an individual's physical, cognitive and emotional energy in work performance.

Kahn's conceptualisation of personal engagement would be the only literature on engagement until early 2001, when Maslach et al. (2001) began understanding why employees developed job burnout. The burnout-antithesis approach is the second significant definition of engagement and defines engagement as the opposite or positive antithesis of burnout (Saks and Gruman 2014). According to Maslach and Leiter (2008, p. 498), engagement is the direct opposite of burnout and engagement is defined as "an energetic state of involvement with personally fulfilling activities that enhance one's sense of professional efficacy". Schaufeli et al. (2002, p. 47) argued that burnout and engagement are independent states, while maintaining that engagement is the opposite of burnout and defined engagement as a "positive, fulfilling, work-related state of mind that is characterised by vigor, dedication and absorption". Kahn (1990) and Maslach et al. (2001) provided the earliest theoretical frameworks for understanding employee engagement and many of the contemporary conceptualisations of engagement are created from their original works (Shuck and Wollard 2009).

The only study to empirically test Kahn's model, May et al. (2004) found that all three of Kahn's (1990) original domains—meaningfulness, safety and availability—were significantly related to engagement. This finding suggests "that the framework Kahn (1990) used in his conceptualization is foundational for the scaffolding of the construct" (Shuck and Wollard 2009, p. 99).

Harter et al. (2002) published one of the earliest consulting articles on employee engagement. Harter et al. (2002) drew data from a meta-analysis of business units across multiple fields of industry and was the first to study employee engagement at a business unit level (Shuck and Wollard 2009). Harter et al. (2002, p. 417) defined employee engagement as an "individual's involvement and satisfaction with as well as enthusiasm for work".

This definition added the expectation of an individual's satisfaction level and altered the way engagement had been previously viewed (Shuck and Wollard 2010). The satisfaction-engagement approach was primarily designed as a management tool to improve job performance, but also had a significant impact in academia as it established meaningful links between employee engagement and business unit outcomes (Schaufeli 2013). This article was the trigger for the rapid expansion of interest in the concept of employee engagement, as it was the first publication that suggested an employee engagement-profit link (Shuck and Wollard 2009).

The first academic research to conceptualise and test antecedents and consequences of employee engagement was conducted in 2006 by Saks (2006). According to Saks (2006) as cited in (Shuck and Wollard 2009), a stronger theoretical rationale for explaining employee engagement can be found in social exchange theory (SET). Saks (2006) was the first to separate job engagement and organisational engagement into separate types of employee engagement. As a result, Saks (2006) defined employee engagement as a "distinct and unique construct that consists of cognitive, emotional, and behavioural components that are associated with individual role performance" (Saks 2006, p. 602). This definition is similar to that of Kahn (1990) as it also focused on role performance at work. This literature, according to Shuck and Wollard (2009), encompassed previous notions that employee engagement was developed from cognitive (Kahn 1990; Maslach et al. 2001), emotional (Harter et al. 2002; Kahn 1990) and behavioural (Harter et al. 2002; Maslach et al. 2001) components. Saks (2006) provided an important bridge between early theories of employee engagement, practitioner literature, and the academic community and was the first to propose an empirical model (Shuck & Wollard 2009).

The Society for Human Resources Management (SHRM) commissioned a publication on employee engagement in 2006 with the aim of making the concept of employee engagement more accessible to SHRM members (Shuck and Wollard 2009). Shuck and Wollard (2009) in their critique of the publication stated that although the publication touched on key engagement concepts it was not clear and concise and lacked a single definition of employee engagement. Shuck and Wollard (2009), however, view the publication as notable as it marked the arrival of professional bodies into the employee engagement conversation.

Two years after the SHRM study, the American Society for Training and Development (ASTD) commissioned a study in association with Dale

Carnegie Training to explore employee engagement further (Shuck and Wollard 2009). This study focused on the role of learning in the employee engagement construct, marking the first major research into the construct from a training perspective (Shuck and Wollard 2009). ASTD defined engagement as "employees who are mentally and emotionally invested in their work and in contributing to their employer's success" (Shuck and Wollard 2009). The results of the study showed a nexus with the "foundational work of Kahn (1990) and Maslach et al. (2001) by creating meaningful work environments, providing opportunities for learning, and focusing on the experience of the employee" (Shuck and Wollard 2009, p. 136).

Building on the work of multiple researchers, Macey and Schneider (2008) pioneered conceptual research in employee engagement. Macey and Schneider (2008) theorise that employee engagement develops from trait engagement, psychological state engagement, and behavioural engagement. Macey and Schneider (2008) drew from previous research and defined each as a separate engagement construct. From Macey and Schneider's (2008, p. 25) perspective, employee engagement is defined by suggesting that "job design attributes would directly affect trait engagement, the presence of a transformational leader would directly affect state engagement, and the presence of a transformational leader would directly affect trust levels and thus, indirectly affect behavioural engagement". In this theoretical model, the preceding state of engagement would build on the next, each developing a piece of the overall employee engagement construct (Shuck and Wollard 2009). This contribution, which built on the work of Saks (2006), helped to clear the vague conceptual state of employee engagement by breaking the engagement construct into distinct parts, namely job engagement and organisation engagement (Shuck and Wollard 2009). In a seminal review of the foundations of engagement, Shuck and Wollard (2009) identified the major contributors to the overall development of the employee engagement concept of which an adapted summary appears in Table 2.1.

The Psychology of Employee Engagement

Positive psychology helps us to understand why engaged employees flourish and thrive as research supports the view that engagement is a distinctive positive concept (Youssef-Morgan and Bockorny 2014). Positive psychology was born out of Seligman and Csikszentmihalyi's (2000)

Table 2.1 Seminal works of employee engagement

Article citation/ author	*Year*	*Contribution*	*Definition of engagement*	*Research type*	*Key concepts*
Kahn *The needs satisfying approach*	1990	Published early theoretical framework of personal engagement and disengagement Defined engagement as separate concept Accredited with first application and use of engagement theory to the workplace Conceptualised that psychological conditions of meaningfulness, safety and availability were important to understand the development of engagement	Kahn (1990, p. 694) "Personal engagement as the harnessing of organisation members' selves to their work roles; in engagement, people employ and express themselves physically, cognitively and emotionally during role performance"	Empirical: Ethnographic research	Physical, cognitive and emotional presence during role performance
Maslach et al. *The burnout-antithesis approach*	2001	The first major work on employee engagement after Kahn (1990) It is, besides the needs satisfying approach, the other early developmental theory on employee engagement Maslach et al. (2001) conceptualised engagement as the positive antithesis to burnout	Maslach and Leiter (2008, p. 498) defined employee engagement as an "energetic states of involvement with personally fulfilling activities that enhance one's sense of professional efficacy" Schaufeli et al. (2002, p. 47) defined engagement as a "positive, fulfilling, work-related state of mind that is characterised by vigor, dedication and absorption"	Conceptual	Maslach Energy, involvement and efficacy Schaufeli Vigor, dedication and absorption

(*continued*)

Table 2.1 (continued)

Article citation/ author	*Year*	*Contribution*	*Definition of engagement*	*Research type*	*Key concepts*
Harter et al. *The satisfaction-engagement approach*	2002	Published first study linking between employee engagement-satisfaction and business unit outcomes (profit) One of the first to mention a profit linkage to employee engagement	Harter et al. (2002, p. 269) defined work engagement "as the individual's involvement and satisfaction with as well as enthusiasm for work"	Empirical: meta-analysis	Business outcomes associated with employee engagement
May et al.	2004	First published empirical research testing Kahn's (1990) conceptualisation of employee engagement	May et al. (2004, p. 12). Engagement is never explicitly defined, though Kahn (1990) referred to	Empirical: survey	Physical, cognitive and emotional expression
Saks *Multidimensional approach*	2006	First explicit research to test antecedents and consequences to employee engagement Prior to Saks (2006), practitioner research was the only body of work connecting employee engagement drivers to employee engagement consequences	Saks (2006, p. 602) defined engagement as "a distinct and unique construct that consists of cognitive, emotional, and behavioural components that are associated with individual role performance"	Empirical: survey	Cognitive, emotional and behavioural components

(*continued*)

Table 2.1 (continued)

Article citation/ author	*Year*	*Contribution*	*Definition of engagement*	*Research type*	*Key concepts*
Vance *Multidimensional approach*	2006	Contribution to the HRD field at the Society for Human Resources Management's (SHRM) First major publication on employee engagement and commitment	SHRM Never defined engagement	Conceptual	Commitment
Czarnowsky *Multidimensional approach*	2008	American Society for Training and Development's (ASTD) first major publication on employee engagement	Czarnowsky (2008, p. 6) defined engagement as "Employees who are mentally and emotionally invested in their work and in contributing to their employer's success"	Empirical: survey	Connection to Kahn's (1990) foundational work
Macey and Schneider *Multidimensional approach*	2008	The first to conceptualise trait, state and behavioural engagement as separate but related constructs Presented organisational concepts that might nourish the development of engagement within organisations	Macey and Schneider (2008) *Trait engagement* the "inclination or orientation to experience the world from a particular vantage point" (p. 5) *Psychological state engagement* is defined as an "antecedent to behavioural engagement (encompassing the constructs of satisfaction, involvement, commitment, and empowerment"; (pp. 5–6) *Behavioural engagement* is "define[d] in terms of discretionary effort" (p. 6)	Conceptual	Trait, state and behavioural engagement

Adapted from Shuck and Wollard (2010, pp. 96–97)

research on learned optimism. According to Seligman and Csikszentmihalyi (2000), the aim of positive psychology is to focus on the strengths and positive aspects of flourishing individuals rather than on weaknesses.

Youssef-Morgan and Bockorny (2014) argue that engagement must be understood within a positive paradigm, rather than an extension of negatively orientated models designed for treating pathologies. Engagement measures and their design remain, strongly influenced by positive psychology (Purcell 2014a).

The changing nature of the modern workplace has put the traditional psychological contract under pressure and when the contract is breached, it results in employee cynicism (Cartwright and Holmes 2006). Employee cynicism is characterised by mistrust in the organisation, its management, and objectives (Cartwright and Holmes 2006). Andersson and Bateman (1997) have established a link between cynicism and reduction in organisational citizenship behaviours (OCB), which is a clear indicator of disengagement amongst employees.

Individual employees vary significantly in their level of engagement due to the changing nature of work and excessive demands put on them by organisations to increase profitability (Youssef-Morgan and Bockorny 2014). Varying levels of engagement encourage increased interest in organisations to create an environment that can facilitate employee engagement as the positive impact of engagement on productivity and financial outcomes is well established (Harter et al. 2002). It is in this context that positivity can help enhance employee engagement and facilitate positive business outcomes at various levels of the organisation (Youssef-Morgan and Bockorny 2014).

Kahn (1990) provides the strongest theoretical rationale for understanding the psychology of engagement than any other model, because Kahn (1990) is clear about the psychological conditions that are necessary for engagement as well as the antecedents that are the most important. Kahn's (1990) conceptualisation of engagement is consistent with the increased demands being put on employees to be more physically, emotionally and cognitively available as the nature of work continuously become more demanding.

According to Youssef-Morgan and Bockorny (2014), positivity is not new to psychology or management, as traditional theories and practices have recognised the importance of positivity. Youssef-Morgan and Bockorny (2014) are of the view that to understand positivity and what it has to offer to enhance engagement levels the traditional roots of positivity in psychology and management must be considered. Youssef-Morgan and Bockorny (2014) identified the traditional roots and foundations of positivity as the traditional motivation theories, job satisfaction, job design, positive reinforcement, positive and negative affect, transformational leadership and three recent positive movements with links to engagement as positive psychology, positive organisational scholarship and positive organisational behaviour.

Positivity can affect the workplace and there is a realisation amongst organisations that positive employees promote engagement through various positive mechanisms (Youssef-Morgan and Bockorny 2014). Youssef-Morgan and Bockorny (2014) postulate that positive managers, employees and organisations are necessary for promoting engagement.

The Meaning of Employee Engagement

There continues to be a lack of consensus amongst academics and practitioners regarding the meaning and distinctiveness of employee engagement from other constructs (Saks and Gruman 2014). The existence of these different definitions makes it difficult to determine if efforts to improve engagement are successful as each study examines employee engagement under a different construct (Kumar and Swetha 2011). This inconsistency resulted in a confused approach to understanding and developing strategies around employee engagement within organisations (Shanmugan and Krishnaveni 2012).

Predominant Employee Engagement Definitions

Shuck (2011) conducted an integrative literature review in 2011 to synthesise the state of academic research on employee engagement and identified four approaches to defining engagement, namely the needs-satisfying approach, burnout-antithesis approach, satisfaction-engagement approach and the multidimensional approach.

The needs-satisfying approach was conceptualised by Kahn (1990) and he defined personal engagement as the "harnessing of organisation members' selves to their work roles: in engagement, people employ and express themselves physically, cognitively, emotionally and mentally during role performance" (Kahn 1990, p. 694). According to Kahn (1990), employees can be engaged on one dimension and not on the other and therefore, the more engaged the employee is on each dimension, the higher his or her overall personal engagement. The cognitive aspect of employee engagement concerns employees' belief about the organisation and its leaders, and their working conditions. The emotional aspect concerns how employees feel about the organisation and its leaders, and their working conditions and whether they have a positive or negative attitude towards the organisation and its leaders (Shanmugan and Krishnaveni 2012).

The burnout-antithesis approach is rooted in the occupational health psychology (Schaufeli 2013). Maslach et al. (2001, p. 417) conceptualised employee engagement as "a persistent positive effective-motivational state of fulfilment in employees characterised by high levels of activation and pleasure characterised by high levels of activation and pleasure". According to Maslach and Leiter (1997) (as cited by Schaufeli 2013), engagement and burnout are the positive and negative endpoints of a single continuum. Engagement is specifically characterised by energy, involvement and efficacy, which are considered the direct opposites of the three-burnout dimension, exhaustion, cynicism, and lack of accomplishment (Schaufeli 2013). This means that people who are high on engagement are inevitably low and burned out, and vice versa (Schaufeli 2013).

The satisfaction-engagement approach is rooted in the positive psychology movement of the early 21st century and conceptualised by Harter et al. (2002). Harter et al. (2002), the empirically based Gallup researchers, published one of the earliest and most definitive pieces of practitioner literature on employee engagement and were the first to look at employee engagement at the business unit level. The Gallup researchers defined employee engagement as an "individual's involvement and satisfaction with as well as enthusiasm for work" (Harter et al. 2002, p. 417). Like the definitions of other consultancy firms, the Gallup engagement concept seems to overlap with well-known traditional constructs such as job involvement and job satisfaction (Schaufeli 2013). However, the satisfaction-engagement approach has had a significant impact in academia as well, as Gallup's research has established meaningful links between employee engagement and business unit outcomes (Harter et al. 2002).

The multidimensional approach emerged from a multidimensional perspective of employee engagement conceptualised by Saks (2006) which hypothesised that employee engagement developed through a social exchange model; Saks was the first academic researcher to suggest separate states of engagement, namely job engagement and organisational engagement. Saks (2006, p. 602) defined the multidimensional concept of engagement as "a distinct and unique construct that consists of cognitive, emotional, and behavioural components that are associated with individual role performance". This definition was inclusive previous literature suggesting that employee engagement was developed from cognitive, emotional and behavioural elements and extended current thinking on the topic by developing a three-component model (Shuck 2011). Saks's (2006) view suggests that for absorption to occur, an employee must readily have physical, emotional and psychological resources to complete their work. Conversely, if the organisation fails to provide the resources, individuals are more likely to withdraw and disengage themselves from the roles (Schaufeli 2013). Thus, the amount of cognitive, emotional and physical resources that an individual is prepared to devote in the performance of their work role may depend on the economic and socio-emotional resources received from the organisation (Kumar and Swetha 2011).

Macey and Schneider (2008) extended Saks's (2006) model by proposing an exhaustive synthesis of all elements that have been utilised to define engagement (Schaufeli 2013). Macey and Schneider (2008) suggest that each proceeding state of engagement (cognitive-emotional-behavioural) build on the next, eventually leading to engagement. Macey and Schneider's (2008) theoretical framework offers a series of propositions about trait engagement, psychological state engagement and behavioural engagement. They define trait engagement as a positive view of life and work and that this trait engagement gets reflected in psychological state engagement as an antecedent of behavioural engagement, which they define in terms of discretionary effort (Macey and Schneider, 2008).

Defining Employee Engagement

There are according to Saks and Gruman (2014) two main definitions of engagement in the academic literature, namely Kahn's (1990) and Schaufeli et al.'s (2002). Their definitions have some similarities and overlap, especially in terms of being a motivational state; they also differ in several ways (Saks and Gruman 2014). Kahn's (1990) definition is more encompassing as it includes the notion of personal agency and the argentic self (Cole et al. 2012), he also suggests something more distinct and unique as it pertains to placing the complete self in role. According to Kahn (1990), engagement is also a rational choice in which individuals make decisions about the extent to which they will bring their true selves into the performance of role. According to Saks and Gruman (2014), Kahn's immersive definition and conceptualisation is much deeper and more substantial than provided by Schaufeli et al.'s (2002) definition. The Schaufeli et al.'s (2002) conceptualisation and definition is too similar to burnout, although there is evidence that engagement is distinct from job attitude, and that it calls its distinctiveness into question (Saks and Gruman 2014).

Welbourne and Schlachter (2014) state that as Kahn's (1990) work evolved it took on a somewhat different lens. Kahn's (1990) work has shifted since its original conceptualisation to be less focused on the individual bringing his/her own interests and preferred roles to work and more about making the organisation and work, in general, the central focus (Welbourne and Schlachter 2014). According to Bailey et al. (2015), the shift away from Kahn's socio-psychological construct of personal role engagement is notable. Welbourne and Schlachter (2014) speculate that Kahn's (1990) idea of engagement, focussed on the employee being able to express him/herself at work, became vague over time as Kahn's (1990) definition evolved.

The most important issue in defining engagement is what elements to include and what elements to exclude from the definition of engagement (Schaufeli 2013). Saks (2008) noted in his critique of Macey and Schneider, who present an all-inclusive taxonomy that covers the entire range of concepts that have been associated with engagement, that engagement serves as an "umbrella term" for whatever one wants it to be. Schaufeli (2013, p. 19) proposed a more restrictive model that "considers work engagement as an experienced psychological state which mediates the impact of job resources and personal resources on organisational outcomes".

Common to the various definitions is, however, the view that employee engagement is a desirable condition, has an organisational purpose and brings involvement, commitment, passion, enthusiasm, focus, effort and energy to the workplace, with both attitudinal and behaviour components (Macey and Schneider 2008). It is a mental state that produces certain behaviours.

"Employee engagement" or "engagement" is preferred for purposes of this chapter and the term employee engagement or engagement will be referred to as the engagement construct in this chapter. The reason for choosing employee engagement as a concept is because employee engagement not only refers to the relationship of an employee with his or her work but also includes the relationship with the organisation (Schaufeli 2013). By including the relationship with the organisation, traditional concepts such as organisational commitment and extra-role behaviour are included.

Employee Engagement as a Unique Construct

Engagement, according to Schaufeli (2013), is surrounded by disagreements over its properties since its advent. While it has been hypothesised that engagement is "a distinct and unique construct that consists of cognitive, emotional and behavioural components that are associated with role performance" (Saks 2006, p. 602), when applied to organisational settings, the concept tends to exhibit considerable overlap with other related constructs. The most evident overlap is with job-related attitudes, job behaviour and behavioural intentions, health and well-being, and personality traits (Schaufeli 2013).

Some researchers argue that engagement is similar to work-related constructs such as motivation, job satisfaction and organisational commitment; other researchers believe it be a distinct concept that can be differentiated from behavioural intentions and actual behaviour that reflects an employee's commitment to an organisation and its goals (Macey and Schneider 2008; Maslach et al. 2001; Robinson et al. 2004).

The concept of engagement according to Schaufeli (2013) does not overlap to such an extent with other concepts that they are identical. Engagement reflects a genuine and unique psychological state that employee might experience at work (Schaufeli 2013). According to Rich et al. (2010), all these constructs tend to have an emotional, cognitive and deliberate element in common, therefore the natural overlap between them. Rigg (2013) is of the opinion that one of the main aspects that appear to set engagement apart is the impact of engagement on health outcomes.

Employee Engagement Frameworks

In exploring the literature; it is clear that an engagement framework that links antecedents to individual performance outcomes in a unionised environment is under-explored. The major theoretical frameworks used will be analysed in order to develop a theoretical framework on how to more successfully engage employees in a unionised environment. This theoretical framework will be informed by existing theories and frameworks in the literature that has already been tested and validated and is considered as generally accepted theory in the literature (Grant and Osanloo 2014).

Just as there are several definitions of employee engagement, several theories of engagement exist. Although a unique framework for engagement does not exist, a number of theoretical perspectives have been proposed with each emphasising a different aspect, but cannot be integrated into one overarching conceptual model (Schaufeli 2013).

Four major theoretical approaches, according to Shuck (2011), define the existing state of engagement, namely Kahn's (1990) need-satisfying approach, Maslach et al.'s (2001) burnout-antithesis approach, Harter et al.'s (2002) satisfaction-engagement approach, and Saks's (2006) multidimensional approach. An exploration of the different frameworks follows.

Need-Satisfying Approach

The needs-satisfying approach first proposed the concept of engagement in the workplace (Shuck 2011). The need-satisfying approach was conceptualised by Kahn (1990) as "personal engagement is the simultaneous employment and expression of a person's 'preferred self' in task behaviours that promote connections to work and to others, personal presence, and active full role performances" (Kahn 1990, p. 700). Kahn (1990) assumes that employees become engaged when three psychological conditions or needs are met.

Kahn's model was first tested by May et al. (2004) and found that meaningfulness and, to a lesser degree, safety and availability were positively associated with engagement and the outcome variable intention to turnover. May et al. (2004) also corroborated Kahn's theorising that job enrichment and role fit were positively related to meaningfulness, whereas rewarding co-workers and supportive supervisors were positively related to safety, while adhering to co-worker norms and self-consciousness were negative predictors. Personal resources were positively related to availability, while participation in outside activities was a negative predictor.

In a sample of 245 fire-fighters, using Kahn's framework, Rich et al. (2010) provided empirical evidence that value congruence, perceived organisational support and core self-evaluation were related to employee engagement and that employee engagement was significantly related to the outcome variables, task performance and organisational citizenship behaviour.

Using employees in multiple fields of industry and Kahn's framework, Shuck (2011) suggested that job fit, effective commitment and psychological climate were all significantly related to employee engagement and that employee engagement was significantly related to discretional effort and intention to turnover. Overall, meaningfulness was found to have the strongest relation to different employee outcomes in terms of engagement (Kumar and Swetha 2011).

The needs-satisfying approach therefore "assumes that when the job is challenging and meaningful, the social environment at work is safe, and personal resources are available, the needs for meaningfulness, safety, and availability are satisfied and thus engagement is likely to occur" (Schaufeli 2013, p. 16).

Saks and Gruman (2014) argue that Kahn's (1990) theory is more convincing as it specifies the psychological conditions that lead to engagement as well as the factors that influence each of the psychological conditions. Saks and Gruman (2014) furthermore argue that any theory of employee engagement should include Kahn's (1990) three psychological conditions of meaningfulness, safety and availability.

Burnout-Antithesis Approach

Maslach et al. (2001) pioneered reaching across academic boundaries of employee engagement, conceptualising the concept as the positive antithesis to burnout. According to Maslach et al. (2001), job engagement is an expansion of the burnout construct, noting the engagement is the opposite of burnout. There are, according to Maslach et al. (2001), six areas of work-life that lead to either burnout or engagement. These six areas are workload, control, rewards and recognition, community and social support, perceived fairness and values. Maslach et al. (2001) argue that job engagement is associated with sustainable workload, feelings of choice and control, appropriate recognition and reward, a supportive work community, fairness and justice and meaningful and valued work. According to Maslach et al. (2001), job burnout is the result of miss-matches in six critical areas of organisational life that is considered the major organisational antecedents of burnout. May et al.'s (2004) findings support Maslach et al.'s (2001) view that meaningful and valued work is associated with engagement. This approach suggests that mismatch leads to burnout, while matches lead to engagement (Saks and Gruman 2014).

According to Schaufeli (2013), two schools of thought exist on this matter. The first approach views engagement and burnout as the positive and negative endpoint of a single continuum (Schaufeli 2013). Work engagement is characterised by energy, involvement and efficiency, which are believed to be the direct opposite of the three burnout dimensions, exhaustion, cynicism and lack of accomplishment, respectively (Maslach et al. 2001). The second alternative view considers work engagement as a distinct concept that is negatively related to burnout (Schaufeli 2013). Besides concerns about the distinctiveness from similar constructs, a related problem has been the tendency by some researchers to view engagement as the opposite to burnout (Saks and Gruman 2014).

The Job Demands-Resource Model (JD-R)

Many studies on work engagement used the JD-R model as an explanatory framework, particularly researchers who believe that engagement is the antithesis of burnout (Schaufeli 2013). The model was used to demonstrate that burnout could develop through different processes (Saks and Gruman 2014). First, burnout is the result of high job demands, which leads to exhaustion. Second, a lack of job resources leads to disengagement from work (Saks and Gruman 2014). The model assumes that work engagement results from the inherently motivating nature of resources, whereby the following types are distinguished.

The JD-R model postulates that work engagement mediates the relationship between job and personal resources on the one side and positive outcomes on the other side; the motivational process (Schaufeli 2013). On the other hand, a negative process also exists, the so-called health impairment process sparked by high job demand (Schaufeli 2013). When job demands are high, additional effort must be employed to achieve the work goals and to prevent decreasing performance (Schaufeli 2013). The additional effort comes at a physical and psychological cost, such as fatigue (Schaufeli 2013). When recovery is inadequate or insufficient, employees gradually exhaust themselves and might eventually burn out Schaufeli (2013).

The JD-R model is the only model that specifically postulates that job characteristics may influence employee engagement (Bakker and Demerouti 2007). According to Bakker and Demerouti (2007), the JD-R model provides the best approximation of the relationships among work characteristics, health and well-being. Saks and Gruman (2014) question if the JD-R model is truly a theory of engagement or just a framework for classifying job demands and job resources as the basic premise of the theory is that the more resources an employee has, the more engaged he/she will be.

The Affective Shift Model

Bledow et al. (2011) developed an affective shift model of work engagement according to which work engagement emerges from the dynamic interplay of positive and negative affect. The affective shift model proposes that engagement will only result from the experience of negative affect if a shift to positive affect takes place (Bledow et al. 2011). The affective shift model seeks to explain the observation that work engagement increase and decrease as a person moves through the day, shifting from one task to another and being exposed to various kinds of events during the day (Bledow et al. 2011). This model is based on the assumption that both positive and negatives affect have important functions for work engagement (Bledow et al. 2011). The model proposes that a core mechanism underlying the emergence of high levels of work engagement is a shift from negative to positive affect (Schaufeli 2013). Bledow et al. (2011) argue that it is the dynamic interplay of positive and negative affect at work that produces work engagement. Bledow et al. (2011) refer to "the temporal sequence of negative affect followed by positive affect as an affective shift" (p. 1247). Bledow et al. (2011) clarify it further by stating that the higher the level of negative affect that is experienced and the higher the level of positive affect that follows, the more noticeable is the affective shift. Bledow et al. (2011), however, caution that an affective shift does not imply that people must first experience a negative effect and then only a positive effect as they are not two poles of one dimension, but two dimensions and people can experience both positive and negative affect within a time interval. The significance of this approach is that, for engagement, a shift from negative to positive affect is essential as work engagement implies the presence of positive affect (Bledow et al. 2011).

Social Exchange Theory (SET)

The models of Kahn (1990) and Maslach et al. (2001) indicate the psychological conditions or antecedents that are necessary for engagement, but they do not clarify why individuals will respond to these conditions with varying degrees of engagement (Kumar and Swetha 2011).

According to Saks (2006), a stronger theoretical rationale for explaining employee engagement can be found in SET. SET contends that relationships at work evolve over time into trusting, loyal and mutual commitments as long as all parties involved abide by reciprocity rules (Schaufeli 2013). SET argues that when employees receive particular resources from the organisation they feel obliged to respond in kind to repay the organisation. Saks (2006) argues that one way for individuals to repay their organisation is through engagement. Saks's (2006) view suggests that for absorption to occur, an employee must readily have physical, emotional and psychological resources to complete their work. Conversely, if the organisation fails to provide the resources, individuals are more likely to withdraw and disengage themselves from the roles (Schaufeli 2013). Thus, the amount of cognitive, emotional and physical resources that an individual is prepared to devote in the performance of their work role may depend on the economic and socio-emotional resources received from the organisation (Kumar and Swetha 2011). Kahn's (1990) conceptualising of engagement that employees feel obliged to bring themselves more deeply into their role performance as repayment for the resources they receive from their organisation parallel the Saks (2006) model of engagement.

Only Kahn's framework offers an empirically tested multidimensional, motivational framework reflecting latent conditions on an employee's willingness to engage, which is a limitation of other frameworks (Rich et al. 2010). Crawford et al. (2014, p. 57) state that "although scholars do not always explicitly use this framework to conceptually ground models of engagement, the majority of antecedent constructs studied reflect, to a great extent, these psychological conditions".

Measuring Employee Engagement

According to Macey and Schneider (2008), measuring employee engagement is a smart business strategy to reach business objectives. It allows organisations to track business objectives and develop tools to effectively measure and manage predictors of employee engagement (Lockwood 2007). The lack of consensus surrounding the meaning and definition of engagement also affects how to measure engagement, but do not prevent researchers from measuring engagement (Saks and Gruman 2014). A

Table 2.2 Engagement scales

Rothbard (2001) developed a 9-item scale, consisting of 4 items that measures attention and 5 items that measure absorption
May et al. (2004) developed a 13-item scale based on the three components of Kahn's (1990) definition of engagement. May et al.'s (2004) scale includes 4 items to measure cognitive engagement, 4 items to measure emotional engagement and 5 items to measure physical engagement
Saks (2006) developed a 6-item scale to measure job engagement and a 6-item scale to measure organisational engagement
Rich et al. (2010) developed an 18-item scale that includes 6 items to measure each of Kahn's three dimensions of engagement
Soane et al. (2012) used a shortened version of the scale, which includes 3 items to assess intellectual engagement; affective engagement measures build on Kahn's (1990) approach
Stumpf et al. (2013) developed a two-dimensional measure of engagement for professionals in technically orientated work groups that measures felt engagement and behavioural engagement
Schaufeli and Bakker (2004) developed the Utrecht Work Engagement Scale (UWES) that consists of 17 items measuring the vigour, dedication and absorption dimensions

wide range of different scales are subsequently in existence to measure engagement (Fletcher and Robinson 2014). Welbourne and Schlachter (2014) state that it is impossible to determine how many measurements exist as the number of practitioners continuously changes and their models are considered propriety and are not published. There are, however, more established methods of measurements.

At least seven different scales have been developed to measure engagement, not including surveys that measure management practices and burnout (Saks and Gruman 2014). The seven most prominent scales identified by Saks and Gruman (2014) are illustrated in Table 2.2.

Most of the measures are based on Kahn's (1990) definition of engagement and the Utrecht Work Engagement Scale, whilst the other measures have seldom been used (Saks and Gruman 2014).

References

Andersson, L. M., & Bateman, T. (1997). Cunicism in the workplace: Some causes and effects. Journal of Organizational Behavior, 18(5), 449–469.

Bailey, C., Madden, A., Alfes, K., & Fletcher, L. (2015). The meaning, antecedents and outcomes of employee engagement: A narrative synthesis. International Journal of Management Reviews, 00, 1–23. doi:https://doi.org/10.1111/ijmr.12077

Bakker, A. B., & Demerouti, E. (2007). The Job Demands-Resources model: stat of the art. Journal of Managerial Psychology, 22(3), 309–328.

Bersin, J. (2015). Becoming irresistible: A new model for employee engagement. Deloitte.

Bhuvanaiah, T., & Raya, R. (2014, October–December). Employee engagement: Key to organisational success. SCMS Journal of Indian Management, 61–71.

Bledow, R., Schmitt, A., Frese, M., & Kuhnel, J. (2011). The affective shift model of work engagement. American Psychological Association, 96(6), 1246–1257.

Cartwright, S., & Holmes, N. (2006). The meaning of work: The challenge of regaining employee engagement and reducing cynicism. Human resources management review, 16, 199–208. doi: https://doi.org/10.1016/j.hrmr.2006.03.012

Cole, M. S., Walter, F., Bedeian, A. G., & O'Boyle, B. L. (2012). Job burnout and employee engagement: A meta-analytic examination of construct proliferation. Journal of Management (38), 1550–1581.

Crabtree, S. (2006, May). Can Managers Engage Unionized Employees? The Gallup Management Journal. Retrieved from http://www.gmj.gallup.com

Crawford, E. R., Rich, B. L., Buckman, B., & Bergeron, J. (2014). The antecedents and drivers of employee engagement. In C. Truss, R. Delbridge, K. Alfes, A. Shantz, & E. Soane, Employee engagement in theory and practice (pp. 57–81). New York: Routledge.

Czarnowsky, M. (2008). Learning's role in employee engagement: An ASTD research Study. Alexandria, VA: American Society for Training & Development.

Fletcher, L., & Robinson, D. (2014). Measuring and understanding employee engagement. In C. Truss, R. Delbridge, K. Alfes, A. Shantz, & E. Soane, Employee engagement in theory and practice (pp. 273–289). New York: Routledge.

Goffman, E. (1959). The presentation of self in everyday life (1st ed.). New York: Doubleday.

Grant, C., & Osanloo, A. (2014). Understanding, selecting, and integrating a theoretical framework in dissertation research: Creating the blueprint for your "house". Administrative Issues Journal, Connecting Education, Practice, and Research, 4(2), 12–25.

Harter, J. K., Schmidt, F. L., & Hayes, T. L. (2002). Business-unit-level relationship between employee satisfaction, employee engagement, and business outcomes: A meta-analysis. Journal of Applied Psychology, 87(2), 268–279.

Kahn, W. A. (1990). Psychological conditions of personal engagement and disengagement at work. Academy of Management Journal, 33(4), 692–724.

Kumar, P., & Swetha, G. (2011). A prognostic examination of employee engagement from its historical roots. International Journal of Trade, Economics and Finance, 2(3), 232.

Lockwood, N. R. (2007). Leveraging Employee Engagement for Competitive Advantage: HR's Strategic Role. Society for Human Resources Management, 1–11.

Macey, W., & Schneider, B. (2008). The Meaning of Employee Engagement. Industrial and Organizational Psychology, 3–30.

Maslach, C., & Leiter, M. P. 1997. The truth about burnout. San Francisco, CA: Jossey-Bass.

Maslach, C., & Leiter, M. P. (2008). Early predictors of job burnout and engagement. Journal of Applied Psychology, 93(3), 498–512.

Maslach, C., Schaufeli, W. B., & Leiter, M. P. (2001). Job burnout. Annual Review of Psychology, 52, 397–422.

May, D. R., Gilson, R. L., & Harter, L. M. (2004). The psychological conditions of meaningfulness, safety and availability and the engagement of the human spirit at work. Journal of Occupational Organisational Psychology, 77, 11–37.

Purcell, J. (2014a). Provocation series paper: Disengaging from engagement. Human Resources Management Journal, 24(3), 241–254.

Rich, B. L., Lepine, J. A., & Crawford, E. R. (2010). Job engagement: Antecedents and effects on job performance. Academy of Management Journal, 53(3), 614–635.

Rigg, J. (2013). Worthwhile Concept or Old Wine? A Review of Employee Engagement and Related Constructs. American Journal of Business and Management, 2(1), 31–36. doi:https://doi.org/10.11634/216796061302229

Robinson, D., Perryman, S., & Hayday, S. (2004). The drivers of employee engagement. Institute of employment studies. Brighton: Institute of employment studies.

Rothbard, N. P. (2001). Enriching or Depleting? The Dynamics of Engagement in Work and Family Roles. Administrative Science Quarterly, 46 (4), 655–684. https://doi.org/10.2307/3094827

Saks, A. M. (2006). Antecedents and consequences of employee engagement. Journal of Managerial Psychology, 21(7), 600–619.

Saks, Alan M., (2008). The Meaning and Bleeding of Employee Engagement: How Muddy Is the Water?. Industrial and Organizational Psychology, 1(01), 40–43.

Saks, A. M., & Gruman, J. A. (2014). What do we really know about employee engagement. Human Resources Development Quarterly, 25(2), 155–182.

Schaufeli, W. (2013). Employee Engagement in Theory and Practice (C. Truss, K. Alfes, R. Delbridge, A. Shantz, & E. Soane, Eds.). London: Routledge.

Schaufeli, W. B., & Bakker, A. B. (2004). Job demands, job resources, and their relationship with burnout and engagement: A multi-sample study. Journal of Organizational Behavior, 25, 293–437. https://doi.org/10.1002/job.248

Schaufeli, W. B., Salanova, M., Gonzalez-Roma, V., & Bakker, A. B. (2002). The measurement of engagement and burnout: A two sample comfirmatory factor analytic approach. Journal of Happiness Studies, 3, 71–92.

Seligman, M. E., & Csikszentmihalyi, M. (2000, January). Positive psychology an introduction. American Psychologist, 55(1), 5–14.

Shanmugan, A., & Krishnaveni. (2012). Employee Engagement: An Introspection. International Journal of Social Science & Interdisciplinary Research, 1(9), 186–195.

Shuck, B. (2011, June). Integrative literature review: Four emerging perspectives of employee engagement: An integrative literature review. Human Resources Development Review, 10(3), 304–328. Retrieved from http://hrd.sagepub.com/content/10/3/304

Shuck, B., & Wollard, K. (2010). Employee engagement and HRD: A seminal review of the foundations. Human Resources Development Review, 9(1), 89–110.

Shuck, M. B., & Wollard, K. K. (2009). A historical perspective of employee engagement: An emerging definition. In M. S. Plakhotnic, S. M. Nielsen, & D. M. Pane (Ed.), Proceedings of the Eighth Annual College of Education & GSN Research Conference (pp. 133–139). Miami: Florida International University. Retrieved from http://coeweb.fiu.edu/research_conference

Soane, E., Truss, K., Alfes, K., Shantz, A., Rees, C., & Gatenby, M. (2012). Development and application of a new measure of employee engagement: the ISA engagement scale. Human resource development international, 15(5), 529–547.

Stumpf, A. S., Tymon, G. W., & van Dam, H. N. (2013, May). Felt and behavioural engagement in workgroups of professionals. Journal of vocational behavior, 255–264.

Vance, R. J. (2006). Employee engagement and commitment: A guide to understanding, measuring, and increasing engagement in your organization. Alexandria, VA: The SHRM Foundation.

Welbourne, T. M., & Schlachter, S. (2014). Engaged in what? Virginia: The Incentive Research Foundation.

Whittington, J., Meskelis, S., Asare, E., & Beldona, S. (2017). Enhancing Employee Engagement: An Evidence-Based Approach. Cham, Switzerland: Palgrave Macmillan.

Youssef-Morgan, C. M., & Bockorny, K. M. (2014). Engagement in the context of positive psychology. In C. Truss, R. Delbridge, K. Alfes, A. Shantz, & E. Soane, Employee engagement in theory and practice (pp. 37–56). New York: Routledge.

CHAPTER 3

Antecedents and Outcomes Associated with High Levels of Engagement

Abstract Employee engagement is an emerging concept in the literature which demonstrates organisational benefits, yet little is known about the antecedents of engagement in a unionised environment. The purpose of this chapter is to identify the researched and validated antecedents of, and outcomes of, engagement through a systematic review of the literature that will have the greatest potential to increase the levels of engagement in a unionised environment. The synthesis of the results shows that engagement is considered a mediating variable in which antecedents influence engagement levels and engagement in turn leads to individual and organisational outcomes (Saks and Gruman, Hum Resour Dev Q 25(2): 155–182, 2014). Job resources, individual psychological states, leadership and a positive perception of the organisation have emerged from the synthesis as having a strong impact on the outcomes of engagement (Bailey et al., The meaning, antecedents and outcomes of employee engagement: A narrative synthesis. Int J Manag Rev 00: 1–23. doi:10.1111/ijmr.12077, 2015).

Keywords Antecedents of engagement • Individual and organisational outcomes • Levels of engagement • Mediating variable • Outcomes of engagement

J. H. Nel, B. Linde, *The Art of Engaging Unionised Employees*,
https://doi.org/10.1007/978-981-13-2197-9_3

Antecedents of Engagement

This chapter identifies the researched and validated antecedents of, and outcomes of, engagement through a systematic review of the literature that has the potential to increase the levels of engagement in a unionised environment.

Organisations believe by managing a range of variables, known as antecedents of engagement, they can effectively manage the consequences of engagement and increase the engagement levels of its employees (Scarlett 2013).

Wollard and Shuck (2011) defined antecedents of employee engagement "as constructs, strategies, or conditions that precede the development of employee engagement and that come before and organisation or manager reaps the benefits of engagement related outcomes" (p. 432).

Antecedents to engagement should be in place before organisations can reap the benefit of an engaged workforce (Rich et al. 2010; Saks 2006) (as cited in Wollard and Shuck 2011). However, identifying which variables enable engagement behaviour is almost as difficult as identifying one single definition of engagement (Macey and Schneider 2008). This is mainly because within the practitioners' and academic literature a multitude of different engagement drivers has been suggested (Robertson-Smith and Markwick 2009).

A great deal of research has been conducted on what drives high levels of engagement in organisations, yet no research has been done focusing on the antecedents which will increase the engagement levels of employees in a unionised environment. Increasing the levels of engagement of employees in a unionised environment has become a priority for organisations as industrial action by workers is on the increase. Employers have embraced employee engagement and view it as a framework for their wider employee relations strategies to manage employee relations in difficult times. The purpose of analysing the data on the antecedents and outcomes of engagement is to determine which approaches and interventions that are already researched and validated have the greatest potential to create high levels of engagement in a unionised environment. The key antecedents associated with higher levels of engagement that will emerge from the review of the literature will be included in the theoretical framework to address the low levels of engagement in a unionised environment. Additional antecedents that will unfold from the literature will be utilised to close the gap in the knowledge base when developing the framework to address the low levels of engagement in a unionised environment.

Engagement is generally considered a mediating variable in which antecedent variables influence engagement, and engagement then leads to work outcomes and mediates the relationship between antecedent variables and work outcomes (Saks and Gruman 2014). Since it is generally accepted that engagement has a positive effect on business outcomes, practitioners and researchers hypothesise what key engagement drivers can be leveraged to bring about increases in employee engagement (Crawford et al. 2014). This has led to an increase in research into factors like job design, leadership, organisational and supervisor support and human resources management practices (Crawford et al. 2014).

Kahn's (1990) foundational theory on the psychological conditions of engagement explains how antecedents' factors link with engagement through the three psychological conditions of meaningfulness, safety and availability. Each of Kahn's (1990) psychological conditions has a distinct set of job resources and job demands that influence it. Bailey et al. (2015) conducted a narrative synthesis on the antecedents and outcomes of employee engagement and found that the strongest link between positive antecedents and high engagement levels was in the area of job resources. This supported Saks and Gruman's (2014) view that various job resources, such as autonomy and performance feedback as well as a supportive environment, have frequently been found to be positively related to engagement. In addition to job resources and job demands, leadership is also believed to play an important role in the engagement process (Macey and Schneider 2008; Bailey et al. 2015).

Bailey et al. (2015) also found a link between individual psychological states, management practices, individual perceptions of the organisation, team and high engagement levels. Organisational interventions and activities had a weaker impact on engagement and job demands showed the lowest correlation with engagement, while hindrance demands are negatively related (Bailey et al. 2015; Saks and Gruman 2014).

Kular et al. (2008) suggest that despite the existence of common engagement drivers, different groups and individuals are influenced by different factors. The complexity of the concept was further proved in that some researchers suggest that aspects in the workplace produce engagement, whilst others suggest that engagement is something that the individual brings to the workplace (Kular et al. 2008). Antecedents identified by various authors are summarised in Table 3.1.

The antecedents of engagement can be grouped under two main headings, namely individual antecedents and organisational-level antecedents.

Table 3.1 Antecedents associated with high levels of engagement

Author	*Antecedents*
Kahn (1990)	Meaningfulness
	Job challenge
	Autonomy
	Variety
	Feedback
	Fit
	Opportunities for development
	Reward and recognition
	Psychological safety
	Social support
	Transformational leadership
	Leader-member exchange
	Workplace climate
	Organisational justice
	Job security
	Psychological availability
	Role overload
	Work-role conflict
	Family-work conflict
	Resource inadequacies
	Time urgency
	Off-work recovery
	Disposition
	Personal Resources
Maslach et al. (2001)	Sustainable workload
	Feelings of choice and control
	Recognition and reward
	Supportive work community
	Fairness and justice
	Meaningful and valued work
Holbeche and Springett (2003)	Meaning
May et al. (2004)	Meaningfulness
	Job enrichment
	Work-role fit
	Safety
	Rewarding co-workers
	Supportive supervisor
	Availability
	Resources
	Adherence to co-worker norms, self-consciousness and outside activities are negative predictors
Saks (2006)	Social exchange involving reciprocity or repayment

(*continued*)

Table 3.1 (continued)

Author	*Antecedents*
Macey and Schneider (2008)	Individual differences
Xanthopoulou et al. (2009)	Job resources and personal resources
Macey et al. (2009)	Have the capacity to engage Have a reason or motivation to engage Have the freedom to engage Know how to engage
Rich et al. (2010)	Value congruence Perceived organisational support Core self evaluations
Christian et al. (2011)	Task variety Transformational leadership Leader-member exchange Conscientiousness Positive affect
Bledow et al. (2011)	Shift from negative to positive affect
Kumar and Swetha (2011)	Individual characteristics
Bakker and Demerouti (2007)	Job design (job demands-resource model, JDR)

Wollard and Shuck (2011, p. 433) defined individual antecedents were defined as "constructs, strategies, and conditions that were applied directly to or by individual employees and that were believed to be foundational to the development of employee engagement". Wollard and Shuck (2011, p. 433) defined organisational-level antecedents as "constructs, strategies, and conditions that were applied across an organisations as foundational to the development of employee engagement and the structural or systematic level".

The literature suggests that negative antecedents such as dysfunctional leadership, poor communication, continuous quality improvement efforts, defiant behaviour, hindrance demand, bullying, adherence to co-worker norms, self-consciousness and abusive supervision are associated with lower levels of engagement (Bailey et al. 2015; Crawford et al. 2014).

Wollard and Shuck (2011) state that it is clear from exploring and examining the various antecedents that antecedents are not process dependant, but rather functions that guide the conditions for high engagement to develop. Wollard and Shuck (2011) conclude that no one process model fit across all antecedents and different organisations would create engagement in different ways, using different organisational specific strategies and methods.

Outcomes of Engagement

One of the reasons that employee engagement has received considerable attention is that it is believed to be associated with important employee and organisational outcomes (Saks and Gruman 2014). Empirical evidence suggests that high levels of engagement can lead to enhanced employee performance (Yalabik et al. 2013; Christian et al. 2011; Rich et al. 2010; Macey and Schneider 2008; Holbeche and Springett 2003; Harter et al. 2002). Higher levels of engagement reduce turnover intention, enhance job performance, task performance, organisational citizenship behaviour, productivity, discretionary effort, commitment and customer service (Wollard and Shuck 2011). High levels of engagement, in turn, have been associated with higher profitability, revenue generation, organisational growth and employee satisfaction. Although neither Kahn (1990) nor May et al. (2004) included outcomes in their studies, Kahn (1990) suggested that high levels of engagement lead to both positive outcomes for individuals as well as organisations.

Many consulting firms have claimed that a link exists between high levels of employee engagement and business success, of which the most convincing evidence for the link comes from studies that have been conducted by the Gallup organisation Schaufeli (2013) BlessingWhite and Kenexa (Bhuvanaiah and Raya 2014).

A meta-analysis conducted by Harter et al. (2002) revealed that levels of engagement are positively related to indicators of business-unit performance, such as customer satisfaction and loyalty, profitability, productivity, turnover and safety. The Harter et al. (2002) meta-analysis confirms the connection between engagement and business results, however, they reiterate that engagement is an individual-level construct and if it does lead to business results, it must first impact individual-level outcomes. It is the Harter et al. (2002) meta-analysis that inspired organisations in creating an engaged workforce.

Macey et al. (2009) found that in a sample of 65 firms from different industries, the top 25% on an average index had greater return on assets (ROA), profitability, and more than double the shareholder value compared to the bottom 25% of firms.

In a narrative synthesis of literature, Bailey et al. (2015) found that there was a strong correlation between engagement and job satisfaction and organisational commitment, a moderate correlation between engagement and turnover intention and burnout, and a weaker correlation between engagement and life satisfaction and general health.

As shown in Table 3.2, positive outcomes associated with employee engagement are numerous and varied. Welbourne and Schlachter (2014) are of the view that this is the case because of different measurement tools used to assess engagement and the numerous definitions used to create those measurement systems. Welbourne and Schlachter (2014) suggest that although there is not enough high-quality data to confirm that engagement alone drives organisational performance, there is enough data to show that engagement is better than disengagement.

Practitioners and academics tend to agree that the consequences of employee engagement are positive, as employees' active commitment and involvement is imperative in the organisational performance and competitive advantage of any organisation.

Cost of Engagement

George (2011) is of the opinion that high engagement levels might not necessarily be a win-win situation for all involved and questions to what extent high engagement is always a constructive experience for employees. George (2011, p. 53) states that "the costs of high work engagement for employees deserve far greater attention than they have received to date and questions to what extent high engagement is always such a positive

Table 3.2 Positive outcomes associated with engagement

Author	*Positive outcomes*
Christian et al. (2011)	Enhanced task performance
Schaufeli (2013)	Organisational commitment
Alfes et al. (2013)	Innovative work behaviour
Harter et al. (2002)	Enhanced business performance
Bakker et al. (2012)	In-role performance
Bakker and Xanthopoulou (2013)	Creativity
Xanthopoulou et al. (2009)	Daily work performance
Rich et al. (2010)	Organisational citizenship behaviour
Salanova et al. (2005)	Service climate and customer loyalty
Shantz et al. (2013)	Individual task performance
Soane et al. (2012)	Turnover intention
Torrente et al. (2012)	Unit-level team performance
Xanthopoulou et al. (2009)	Financial returns
Hakanen et al. (2008)	In-role and extra-role performance
Yalabik et al. (2013)	Job performance

experience for employees". George (2011) cites rising levels of productivity associated with work intensification and income inequality, and questions the legitimacy of organisations deliberately soliciting high engagement levels but failing to reward workers appropriately.

Halbesleben (2011) in his commentary on engagement supports George's (2011) view that there is a strong possibility that engaged employees will experience an impaired work–life balance, family relationships and job crafting.

Truss et al. (2013) also note that little consideration has been given to equality and diversity in relation to engagement and that the literature remains silent on how engagement interacts with gender and ethnicity.

References

Alfes, K., Truss, C., Soane, E. C., Rees, C., & Gatenby, M. (2013, November–December). The relationship between line manager behavior, perceived HRM practices, and individual performance: Examining the mediating role of engagement. Human Resources Management, 52(6), 839–859.

Bailey, C., Madden, A., Alfes, K., & Fletcher, L. (2015). The meaning, antecedents and outcomes of employee engagement: A narrative synthesis. International Journal of Management Reviews, 00, 1–23. doi:https://doi.org/10.1111/ijmr.12077

Bakker, A. B., & Demerouti, E. (2007). The Job Demands-Resources model: state of the art. Journal of Managerial Psychology, 22(3), 309–328.

Bakker, A. B., Demerouti, E., & Lieke, L. (2012). Work engagement, performance, and active learning: The role of conscientiousness. Journal of Vocational Behavior, 80(2), 555–564.

Bakker, A. B., & Xanthopoulou, D. (2013). Creativity and charisma among female leaders: the role of resources and work engagement. International Journal of Human Resource Management, 24, 2670–2779.

Bates, S. (2004). Getting engaged. HR Magazine

Bhuvanaiah, T., & Raya, R. (2014, October–December). Employee engagement: Key to organisational success. SCMS Journal of Indian Management, 61–71.

Bledow, R., Schmitt, A., Frese, M., & Kuhnel, J. (2011). The affective shift model of work engagement. American Psychological Association, 96(6), 1246–1257.

Christian, M. S., Garza, A. S., & Slaughter, J. E. (2011). Work engagement: A qualitative review and test of its relations with task and contextual performance. Personnel Psychology, 64, 89–136.

Crawford, E. R., Rich, B. L., Buckman, B., & Bergeron, J. (2014). The antecedents and drivers of employee engagement. In C. Truss, R. Delbridge, K. Alfes, A. Shantz, & E. Soane, Employee engagement in theory and practice (pp. 57–81). New York: Routledge.

George, J. M. (2011). The wider context, costs and benefits of work engagement. European Journal of Work and Organizational Psychology, 20(1), 53–59.

Hakanen, J. J., Schaufeli, W. B., & Ahola, K. (2008). The Job Demands-Resources model: A three-year cross-lagged study of burnout, depression, commitment, and work engagement. Work & Stress 22(3), 224–241.

Halbesleben, J. R. (2011). The consequences of engagement: The good, the bad, and the ugly. European journal of work and organizational psychology, 20(1), 68–73.

Harter, J. K., Schmidt, F. L., & Hayes, T. L. (2002). Business-unit-level relationship between employee satisfaction, employee engagement, and business outcomes: A meta-analysis. Journal of Applied Psychology, 87(2), 268–279.

Holbeche, L., & Springett, N. (2003). In Search of Meaning in the Workplace. Horsham: Roffey Park.

Kahn, W. A. (1990). Psychological conditions of personal engagement and disengagement at work. Academy of Management Journal, 33(4), 692–724.

Kular, S., Gatenby, M., Rees, C., Soane, E., & Truss, K. (2008). Employee Engagement: A Literature Review. Surrey: Kingston University.

Kumar, P., & Swetha, G. (2011). A prognostic examination of employee engagement from its historical roots. International Journal of Trade, Economics and Finance, 2(3), 232.

Macey, W. H., Schneider, B., Barbera, K. M., & Young, S. A. (2009). Employee Engagement: Tools for Analysis, Practice, and Competitive Advantage (First Edition ed.). Chichester West Sussex: Wiley-Blackwell.

Macey, W., & Schneider, B. (2008). The Meaning of Employee Engagement. Industrial and Organizational Psychology, 3–30.

Maslach, C., Schaufeli, W. B., & Leiter, M. P. (2001). Job burnout. Annual Review of Psychology, 52, 397–422.

May, D. R., Gilson, R. L., & Harter, L. M. (2004). The psychological conditions of meaningfulness, safety and availability and the engagement of the human spirit at work. Journal of Occupational Organisational Psychology, 77, 11–37.

Rich, B. L., Lepine, J. A., & Crawford, E. R. (2010). Job engagement: Antecedents and effects on job performance. Academy of Management Journal, 53(3), 614–635.

Robertson-Smith, G., & Markwick, C. (2009). Employee Engagement: A review of current thinking. University of Sussex. Brighton: Institute for Employment Studies.

Saks, A. M. (2006). Antecedents and consequences of employee engagement. Journal of Managerial Psychology, 21(7), 600–619.

Saks, A. M., & Gruman, J. A. (2014). What do we really know about employee engagement. Human Resources Development Quarterly, 25(2), 155–182.

Salanova, M., Agut, S., Peiró, J. M. (2005). Linking Organizational Resources and Work Engagement to Employee Performance and Customer Loyalty: The Mediation of Service Climate. Journal of Applied Psychology 90(6), 1217–1227.

Scarlett, K. (2013, July 30). Scarlett Surveys International. Retrieved July 30, 2013, from http://www.scarlettsurveys.com

Schaufeli, W. B. (2013). What is engagement? In C. Truss, K. Alfes, R. Delbridge, A. Shantz, & E. Soane (Eds.), Employee Engagement in Theory and Practice. London: Routledge.

Shantz, M., Alfes, K., Truss, C., & Soane, E. (2013). The role of employee engagement in the relationship between job design and task performance, citizenship and deviant behaviours. The International Journal of Human Resource Management, 24(13), 2608–2627.

Soane, E., Truss, K., Alfes, K., Shantz, A., Rees, C., & Gatenby, M. (2012). Development and application of a new measure of employee engagement: the ISA engagement scale. Human resource development international, 15(5), 529–547.

Torrente, P., Salanova, M., Llorens, S., & Schaufeli, W.B. (2012). Teams make it work: How teams work engagement mediates between social resources and performance in teams. Psicothema, 24(1), 106–112.

Truss, C., Shantz, A., Soane, E., Alfes, K., & Delbridge, R. (2013). Employee engagement, organisational performance and individual well-being: Exploring the evidence, developing the theory. The International Journal of Human Resources Management, 24(14), 2657–2669.

Welbourne, T. M., & Schlachter, S. (2014). Engaged in what? Virginia: The Incentive Research Foundation.

Wollard, K. K., & Shuck, B. (2011). Antecedents to Employee Engagement: A structured review of the literature. Advances in Developing Human Resources, 13(4), 429–446.

Xanthopoulou, D., Bakker, A., Demerouti, E., & Schaufeli, W. (2009). Work engagement and financial returns: A diary study on the role o f job and personal resources. Journal of Occupational and Organizational Psychology (82), 183–200.

Yalabik, Z. Y., Potaitoon, P., Chowne, J. A., & Rayton, B. A. (2013). Work engagement as a mediator between employee attitudes and outcomes. International Journal of Human Resource Management (24), 2799–2823.

CHAPTER 4

Circumstances That Influence Engagement in a Unionised Environment

Abstract In order to address low levels of engagement in a unionised environment there must be a clear understanding of the circumstances that influence engagement levels in a unionised work environment. In this chapter, the dynamics of the employee-organisation relationship are discussed, in relation to the psychological contract and the employment relationship. The necessity for sound employment relationships and fulfilled psychological contracts are explained as a base for workplace engagement. It confirms that the employment relationship is also exposed to environmental influences, including the labour relations approach of a country with the resulting external labour regulations that need to be applied. The role of collective bargaining and the changed role of trade unions are placed in context with a globalised economic environment with the resulting demands on the employee-organisation relationship.

Keywords Circumstances that influence engagement • Employee-organisational relationship • Employment relationship • Global economic environment • Trade union

The Employee-Organisation Relationship (EOR)

A clear understanding of the nature of the relationship between the employee and the organisation—the employee-organisation relationship (EOR)—is necessary to address low levels of engagement in a unionised

J. H. Nel, B. Linde, *The Art of Engaging Unionised Employees*,
https://doi.org/10.1007/978-981-13-2197-9_4

environment. A stable and sound EOR enhances the possibility for increasing engagement levels, but it is exposed to organisational changes and also functions within the broader labour relations system, as well as the external environment. EOR is the main relationship in the labour relations system that establishes the foundation of the complexity and dynamics of the total labour relations system (Linde 2015). According to Shore et al. (2004), EOR is an overarching term to describe the entire relationship between the employee and the organisation. It includes both micro-concepts—the psychological contract, employee engagement, psychological empowerment and perceived organisational support—and macro-concepts—the employment relationship (Coyle-Shapiro and Shore 2007; Eldor and Vigoda-Gadot 2016). Linde (2015) suggests that the psychological contract and employment relationship are the main concepts of EOR, since the identification and expectation of employment-related promises are identified in the psychological contract, and the implementation and application of employment rules, policies and procedures to maintain these expectations are controlled by the employment relationship.

EOR theory has its roots in the social exchange and inducements-contributions model, which involves a series of interactions that generate obligations to reciprocate (Coyle-Shapiro and Shore 2007). Three aspects are fundamental to social exchange, namely the relationship, reciprocity and exchange (Coyle-Shapiro and Shore 2007). A social exchange relationship starts with one party bestowing a benefit to the other, and if the other party reciprocates, a series of benefits exchange occurs, which creates mutual obligations between these parties.

Evidence presented by Shore et al. (2004) indicates that EOR occurs at multiple levels in the organisation, and has multiple inputs from varying levels, including the job, group and organisation. According to Alcover et al. (2016), various research indicated with extensive empirical evidence that forms of exchange consistently predict a wide range of work-related attitudes and behaviours, such as identification, commitment, psychological attachment, trust, job satisfaction, turnover intentions, organisational citizenship behaviour, work effort and in-role performance. These are all aspects essential to establish a viable environment for employee engagement.

In the next section, the psychological contract and the employment relationship are highlighted as the main concepts of the EOR from an engagement perspective. Linde (2015) proposes that the concepts are discussed separately to take the interdependence of the constructs into account but also states that it is important to note that the two concepts cannot be entirely separated from each other.

The Psychological Contract and Engagement

The employment relationship is the perspective on the exchange relationship with employees, which is institutionalised through the legal employment contract (Lammerts et al. 2017). The formal legal contract only partially reflects the obligated exchanges between employer and employee and does not address all aspects of the employment relationship. This realises since an employment relationship is based on written, verbal and tacit agreements. The inability of the formal written employment contract to fully reflect the mutual agreements of the employment relationship influences the perceived psychological contract, which suggests that there exists an implicit contractual relationship between employer and employee, which is derived from a series of assumptions on both parts about the nature of the relationship. These assumptions, not being formal agreements, constitute a set of reciprocal arrangements and form the basis of a series of expectations that may have a degree of moral force (Leat 2008), forming the perceived psychological contract.

The most widely accepted definition of the psychological contract is that of Rousseau (1995) who defined it as individual beliefs, shaped by the organisation, regarding terms of an exchange arrangement between the individual and their organisation. The psychological contract provides a framework for recognising, interpreting and understanding of implied expectations of employees in the workplace, which extend beyond mere adherence to the terms of a contract of employment (Hall 2015).

Rousseau (1995, p. 112) states that a violation of the psychological contract refers to a failure to comply with the terms of the contract and identifies three sources of experienced violation, being “inadvertent experience, disruption and breach of contract”. The experience of violation is the same, whatever the source. Indicators and reactions of the experience of violation are visible in employee short-term reactions (including job satisfaction levels, job insecurity and trust levels) and long-term reactions (including employee well-being and health) (Linde 2015). Indicators and reactions also include labour-related actions, such as strikes, excessive absenteeism, grievances, disputes and strong union activities. These are important factors to take into account when engagement in the workplace is looked at. An employment relationship with an unbalanced and unfulfilled psychological contract would not create a good relationship to engage employees. This will furthermore create an environment for external influences on engagement levels, since such employment relationships are less controlled internally and more influenced externally. Such external social context influences on the employment relationship are beyond the reasonable control of the organisation and the internal influences are within the reasonable control of organisations. Changes in society and organisations also lead to the change in the psychological contract and the formation of a changed, or even new, psychological contract (van der Smissen et al. 2013). Such a changed psychological contract also needs to be addressed in approaching the engagement of the employees.

Van der Smissen et al. (2013) underline that a shift in the old psychological contract focuses on job security, permanence, loyalty and fairness, whereas the emergent "new" psychological contract focuses on employability and flexibility.

There has been renewed interest in the psychological contract, as with the construct of engagement since the 1990s due to various changes affecting the workplace (Guest and Conway 2002). Hall (2015) mentions that the psychological contract seems closely related to other constructs including employee engagement. Robinson et al. (2004) emphasise the similarity of engagement to the psychological contract in that it is unwritten, reinforced by trust, a reciprocal relationship between employer and employee and easy to break. Guest and Conway (2002) are of the view that the psychological contract can facilitate a new framework for engagement, as the traditional collective model is less relevant in many workplaces. This model can accommodate the rise in individualism and flexibility and can also address the core issues of the employment relationship of trust. Although the relationship between engagement and the psychological contract is unclear, it is postulated by Hall (2015) that high engagement levels require a strong relational contract.

Sisson (2008) states that the psychological contract approach offers, at best, a partial framework for analysing the employment relationship as it deals with an important and often neglected dimension of the employment relationship.

The Employment Relationship and Engagement

According to Shore et al. (2004), the employment relationship is the key relationship between individual employees and employer. Relationships are the nervous system of the organisation in which engagement either thrives or wilts (Kahn and Heaphy 2014). The employment relationship is primarily an exchange relationship whose distinguishing feature is that it involves both monetary and managerial relations (Sisson 2008). Additional features of the relationship are that it is intermediate and incomplete, as many of the benefits that employees receive from the exchange can be set (Sisson 2008). The relationship is furthermore continuous or open-ended in that the relationship is not a one-off exchange as in the case of labour service agreements (Sisson 2008).

The employment relationship differs from other relationships in that it has an economic foundation, often impersonal, and is marked by negative attitudes from both employer and employee (Bendix 2015). The net result is that it is a more complex relationship than other relationships, because its key elements are the simultaneous conflict and common-ground elements that are built into any employment relationship (Nel et al. 2016). The heart of the conflict is built around the economic dimension of the employment relationship, the exchange of labour for monetary reward and employment security (Nel et al. 2016).

The employment relationship is a human one, like other relationships, and what makes those relationships functional promotes a sound employment relationship (Bendix 2015). According to Bendix (2015), the employment relationship improves by mutual interest, mutual support, trust, meaningful communication and shared goals and values. Nel et al. (2016) confirm that the employment relationship is multidimensional with an economic dimension at its core, entailing individual and collective dimensions (trade unions) as well as formal (employment regulations) and informal (the psychological contract) dimensions. However, only respect for individuality in the relationship can lead to personal satisfaction and meaningful relationships (Bendix 2015).

Traditional theory identifies three approaches, ideologies or frames of reference to the employment relationship, namely the unitary, radical and pluralist approaches (Nel et al. 2016). The unitary and radical approaches can be traced to particular ideologies, whilst the pluralist approach constitutes and attempts to achieve a compromise between different ideological positions (Bendix 2015). To these traditional approaches, concertation, corporatism and worker control can be added, as it can be viewed as stemming from the three traditional approaches (Slabbert and Swanepoel 2002).

Creating an Employment Environment for Engagement

Engaging unionised employees requires a thorough understanding of the nature of the employment relationship, as well as the functioning of the broader labour relations system due to its complexity. Dunlop (1958) refers to actors who are involved in the employment (industrial) relationship, which includes a hierarchy of managers and their representatives, non-managerial workers and their spokespersons and government agencies. This is also referred to as the labour tripartite relationship, where these actors operate within the constraints of various environmental influences, parties and power realities, structures and processes for conflict resolution and outcomes. The parties in this relationship establish rules for the workplace and work community through their interaction and within the environmental constraints.

The labour relations system operating in a particular society is a product of that society (Bendix 2015). All the different forces in that society will shape a country's labour relations approach and system in a unique way. Rapid changes in the socio-economic spheres of the society have major impacts on the employment relationship and the features that comprise them. The employer needs to incorporate these environmental influences, through the applied labour relations approach and system, when developing the employment relationship's structure and regulations.

Employment Regulations

The purpose for the employment relationship is the desire on the part of management and employees to exert control over each other. The employer uses rules, policies and procedures as regulations to commit the employee in certain workplace behaviour, associated with the inherent requirements of the relationship. These workplace regulations refer to labour legislation and employment regulations (Linde 2015), which are dynamic and under frequent review to accommodate the changing context and shift in power relations at the workplace.

Linde et al. (2008) developed and tested a model that explains the process of experiencing employment regulations. This model is based on the assumption that for an employee to experience employment regulations positively there should be clarity about the contents of the regulations and the employee must trust the reason for and the application of the regulations. For an employee to have clarity about regulations in the specific employment relationship, the policies, procedures and codes associated with them must be available to the employee, the employee must ascertain the contents of the regulations, and the employee must understand the contents and accept the rule or regulation as fair. These authors (Linde et al. 2008) also confirm the link between clarity in workplace rules, policies and procedures with trust in the management. It is essential for an employer to create a clear and understandable employment relation structure, through internal regulations, to develop a trusting environment where workplace engagement can be increased.

External Influences on the Employment Environment

The employment relationship does not exist in a vacuum (Leat 2008). Delbridge and Keenoy (2010, p. 801) argue that "the practice of management can only be understood in the context of the wider social-economic, political and cultural factors which shape those practices". These factors will therefore influence the way organisations engage their employees and how the unions respond to this. The direct work environment (micro-environment) and the wider society (macro-environment) form a dynamic and complex system that influences the management of work-related relationships. This interaction is demonstrated by the fact that the political system, which is based on a particular approach, will determine the labour relations system, which will internally influence the employment relationship (Bendix 2015; Slabbert and Swanepoel 2002). Labour relations systems that are emerging are based on economic and political pragmatism rather than on ideology alone (Finnemore 2009). Linde (2015) emphasises that the constant change not only influences employment relations, but also transforms a country's socio-political system, its culture, defining values and overall form. The parties consequently exercise their strategic choices within the labour relations processes to respond to impact with the environmental influences (Finnemore 2009).

The Changing Nature of Labour Relations: Opportunities and Challenges for Trade Unions

Most industrialised market economies have in the past decades experienced fundamental, long-term, socio-political and economic changes. Not only have these changes impacted on the way organisations are engaging their employees in a unionised environment, they have also impacted every facet of society. These changes put greater pressure on employees who are challenging the classical views of the employee-organisation relationship. The employee engagement construct is the best positioned one to challenge the requirements of the contemporary employee-organisation relationship (Eldor and Vigoda-Gadot, 2016). The role of the unions has also changed significantly over the past decades. Globalisation, a growing trend in outsourcing, legislative constraints and employer forms of participation have together reduced the influence on unions in the workplace (Wright 2011). The way unions respond to these challenges and opportunities presented by the changing nature of work and employment relations will have to be considered in developing an engagement framework.

Manufacturers demanded an increased production volume until the 1960s, being able to sell everything they produced. The 1970s heralded the era of quality, as high-quality, but low-priced Asian products entered western markets in significant numbers. During the 1980s production capacity exceeded demand and manufacturers offered an ever-widening range of products. In the 1990s the basis of competitive advantage has become even more complex. Today's market place demands that organisations compete on price, quality, innovation, delivery time, customisation and service. This drastic production market change resulted in significant influences on the employment relationship and the role of the trade union, resulting in a new labour relation order.

The Emergence of a New Global Labour Order

Mass production is based on the innovations of Frederick Taylor and Henry Ford (Anstey 1997a). The essential requirement of the mass production system was uninterrupted production of standardised goods in large volumes to meet seemingly insatiable demand, based on a military-style managerial system, hierarchical and bureaucratic and founded on functional specialisation and the division of responsibilities to ensure production. Central to the Taylorist method is job fragmentation, de-skilling and the introduction of specialised sequential repetitive tasks which promote efficiencies and volumes (Anstey 1997a). Assembly line workers were easily unionised as work was repetitive, machine passed, often unsafe, poorly paid and large numbers of workers were located in a single plant making for easier access for union officials. Strikes occurred frequently and employers were compelled by strong unions into bargaining arrangements to solve the conflicts (Finnemore 1996).

What was of global importance was the need for developing new models of production, participation and representation, replacing the traditional institutions. Producer-push mass production systems have internationally been replaced with consumer pull methods which emphasise flexibility in production (Anstey 1997a). Customers increasingly expect to have their individual needs met and quality is rapidly becoming the prerequisite for customer satisfaction. Flexible lean production is characterised by continuous improvement aimed at eliminating waste, flatter structures through number of job grades, education and training of workers, teamwork, job rotation and self-management. Most importantly, the characteristics of the new workforce mandate that organisations must move towards participation. If workers cannot be guaranteed lifetime employment, then at least they want to be involved and have their opinions heard as long as they are in the organisation. One of the most popular forms of work reorganisation is team or group work (Nel 1999).

Globalisation and Employment

These advances had a major impact on labour relations systems in the face of the emergence of a global economy characterised by intense competition (Anstey 1997b). These advances were characterised by global investments, the rise of Asian competition, technological innovation, restructuring of businesses, new forms of work organisations, shift to reduce the role of the state as regulator, and swings in political power away from trade union interests (Anstey 1997b). This led to the internationalisation of trade and capital and the term "globalisation" (Slabbert and Swanepoel 2002). The accelerating challenge of globalisation was the most significant factor influencing the labour relations environment.

Organisations were suddenly subjected to vigorous re-examination and restructuring as a consequence of pressures and new forms of work organisation brought about by globalisation (Finnemore 2009). Employment flexibility, lean manufacturing principles and high levels of engagement have been some responses to pressure induced by the changing economy, individual and organisational realities (Finnemore 2009). The realities of global competition led to changes in the level and nature of employment across nations (Anstey 1997b).

Organisations had to adapt to the realities of the new work order and radical adjustments like the restructuring of organisations as a means of survival in the face of increased competition was required (Finnemore 2009).

In their efforts to achieve competitiveness, organisations have introduced flexibility, which fundamentally affects the nature of work, its organisation, the workforce and the shape of modern business. One of these adjustments was a work paradigm that encouraged enterprises to distinguish between a core of skilled workers and a growing pool of unskilled workers on the periphery of employment who are dispensable (Webster and Buhlungu 2004). Employment has become more volatile and full-time employment is now a decreasing activity (Wickens 1995). Functional flexibility (multiskilling) underpins flexible and more creative use of staff and requires intensive training and development programmes. In addition, there are strong pushes for flexible pay systems linking reward with performance. Privatisation, outsourcing, downsizing, flexible organisations and employment contracts have serious implications for employees, trade unions and traditional collective bargaining (Nel 1999).

The growth of small businesses is accelerating as large companies divest themselves both of non-core activities and of people. The balance between managerial/professional and unskilled jobs is changing in favour of the managerial/professional, although with large companies reducing their middle management ranks, these new positions are likely to be in the more volatile smaller companies. Those who lack the necessary skills to be employable or self-employed will join the growing ranks of the unemployable. The emerging consensus is that the ability to create employment in the established industrialised economies will depend on a balance between high-quality education and training, a dynamic labour market and ease of job creation (Wickens 1995).

Problems for Trade Unions

External factors characterised by intense competition and subsequent pressure on businesses to raise their quality, reduce costs and increase productivity has had a major impact on the nature of work and the employment relationship (Anstey 1997b). These changes have created significant challenges for unions who grapple with the complexity, due to a growing trend in outsourcing and the growth in atypical employment, employer forms of participation and representation, and the imposition of legal constraints on the ability to stay relevant in the workplace (Wright 2011).

The economic slowdown and the decline of manufacturing in these countries have shaken the stability of traditional economies. Trade unions have declined in density as they struggle to respond to internal reshaping imposed by an increasingly service-based membership; to shift strategies from increasing wages to job security through training, development and productivity; to become partners in the struggle for organisational competitiveness; and to deal with the new managerial approaches and technology. The use of the strike weapon has declined across first world countries, as there has been recognition that its use may not be functional in the context of the next world economy (Anstey 1997b).

The new types of disputes are less concerned with the advancement of basic labour rights, power-driven exchanges over wages and conditions of employment and changes on the political front. They are centrally driven by organisational issues and the impact that the changes in these areas have on the nature of work, employment contracts, job security, collective agreements, consultation and collective bargaining processes.

Traditional unions have so far failed to address the marginalisation of workers excluded from union membership, inequality and poverty brought about by globalisation (Webster 2015). Globalisation has proved to be a double-edged sword for unions and employers alike (Finnemore 2009).

The opportunities of foreign investment, new technology, access to global markets have been countered by aggressive competition, financial volatility and the economic meltdown experienced in the global economy in 2008 (Finnemore 2009). This reality led to restructuring, closure of businesses and retrenchments, which placed significant demands on unions (Finnemore 2009). Unions had to devise strategies to deal with the major challenges in terms of political identity and stance, competitiveness, productivity, new forms of work organisation and reshaping of business organisations (Anstey 1997b).

Labour Relations During Political Transitions

The late 1980s and the beginning of the 1990s not only represented fundamental changes in global economics, but also represented a period of fundamental political change for many countries and democratisation appeared to be a world-wide trend (Wood and Coetzee 2006). In protracted transitions all the social role players (state, labour and employer) are forced into a serious of strategic choices (Anstey 1997b). From the beginning of industrialisation, unions have been formed to bring about political transformation in society (Finnemore 2009). Unions historically have done this in three ways, namely forming a labour party, forming an alliance with a chosen party or supporting a party's electoral programme during elections (Buhlungu and Tshoaedi 2012).

Globalisation and the orientation of governments towards neo-liberal policies have severely hampered unions' ability to effectively influence social policy and the way it benefits its broad membership. It is, according to Anstey (1997b), not uncommon for unions to be pulled towards integration into the capitalist society once the political context changes towards the establishment of a democratic state. Unions' response to organisational and political challenges has a marked influence on the labour relations system (Anstey 1997b). In general, unions are struggling to adapt to the new terrain of policy making in the new democracy (Anstey 1997b). This involves more than simply a lack of capacity (Webster 1998). It entails the difficulties of shifting from outright resistance to the state to a subtle combination of opposition with engagement and co-responsibility for particular policies as concertation depends on the capacity of the labour movement to represent its members (Webster 1998).

The changes that occurred in the global economic relations and political systems over the last 40 years shed some light on the ambiguity that organisations need to manage in an attempt to secure worker commitment and motivation. The challenge for organisations is to "balance" these factors as they influence how organisations relate to their employees, and a unions approach to engagement (Tsui et al. 1995). The various internal and external factors that influence engagement levels in a unionised environment are summarised in Table 4.1.

Table 4.1 External factors that influence engagement levels in a unionised environment

External factors	*Internal factors*
Government regulations	Goals and values of employer and employee
Socio-economic, cultural and political situation	Business strategy
History of country	Budgetary factors
Nature of labour force	Organisational structure
Business environment and technology	Ideology
Globalisation	Changing membership
Alliances	Changing nature of trade unions
Trade union climate	Trade union democracy
Political role of trade unions	Job characteristics
	Employment rules and regulations
	Employment relationship
	Role and function of shop stewards
	Psychological contract
	New forms of management

Adapted from Tsui et al. (1995)

References

Alcover, C.-M., Rico, R., Turnley, W. H., & Bolino, M. C. (2016). Understanding the changing nature of psychological contracts in 21st century organisations: A multiple-foci exchange relationships approach and proposed framework. Organizational Psychological Review, 1–32.

Anstey, M. (1997a). Employee Participation and workplace forums. Kenwyn: Juta & Co, Ltd.

Anstey, M. (1997b). Labour Relations in Transition: A changing South Africa in a changing world. Port Elizabeth: Mark Anstey.

Bendix, S. (2015). Labour relations: A southern African perspective (Sixth edition ed.). Cape Town: Juta.

Buhlungu, S., & Tshoaedi, M. (2012). Cosatu's Contested Legacy (First ed.). Cape Town: HSRC Press.

Coyle-Shapiro, J. A.-M., & Shore, L. (2007). The employee-organisational relationship: Where do we go from here? Human Resource Management Review, 17, 166–179.

Delbridge, R., & Keenoy, T. (2010). Beyond managerialism? The International Journal of Human Resource Management, 21(6), 799–817.

Dunlop, J. T. (1958). Industrial Relations System. Carbondale, Illinois: Southern Illinois University Press.

Eldor, L., & Vigoda-Gadot, E. (2016). The nature of employee engagement: rethinking the employee-organization relationship. The International Journal of Human Resource Management, 28, 1–27.

Finnemore, M. (1996). Introduction to labour relations in South Africa (4th ed.). Durban: Butterworths.

Finnemore, M. (2009). Introduction to labour relations in South Africa (Tenth Edition ed.). Durban: LexisNexis.

Guest, D. E., & Conway, N. (2002). Pressure at work and the psychological contract. London: CIPD.

Hall, R. (2015, March 22). Psychological contracts: An introduction to the concept. Retrieved from TAFE NSW: http://www.google.co.za/url?sa=t&rct=j&q=&esrc=s&source=web&cd=1&cad=rja&uact=8&ved=2ahUKEwiQp-zYyOzcAhXpK8AKHRfLCtIQFjAAegQIABAC&url=http%3A%2F%2Flrrpublic.cli.det.nsw.edu.au%2FlrrSecure%2FSites%2FWeb%2F13289%2Fezine%2Fyear_2008%2Fsep%2Fdocuments%2FPsychological-contracts-introduction.doc&usg=AOvVaw0oO4EIZuPHsMSQ0QmdkfLo

Kahn, W. A., & Heaphy, E. D. (2014). Relational context of personal engagement at work. In C. Truss, R. Delbridge, K. Alfes, A. Shantz, & E. Soane, Employee engagement in theory and practice (pp. 83–96). London: Routledge.

Leat, M. (2008). Employee Relations. Edinburgh Business School Heriot-Watt University. Edinburgh, Great Britain: Edinburgh Business School.

Lammerts, L., Van Dongen, J. M., Schaafsma, F. G., Van Mechelen, W., & Anema, J. R. (2017). A participatory supportive return to work program for workers without an employment contract, sick-listed due to a common mental disorder: An economic evaluation alongside a randomized controlled trial. BMC public health, 17(1), 162.

Linde, B. (2015). The value of wellness in the workplace: A perspective of the employee-organisation relationship in the South African labour market. Springer.

Linde, B., Schalk, R., & Linde, H. (2008). Clarity and trust: The experience of workplace regulations by employees. South African Journal of Labour Relations, 32(2), 86–103.

Nel, J. H. (1999). An evaluation of the implementation of a Japanese program for workplace improvement in a South African dairy company. Port Elizabeth: Unpublished Master's degree treatise.

Nel, P., Kirsten, M., Swanepoel, B., Erasmus, B., & Jordaan, B. (2016). South African employment relations: Theory and practice (Eight edition ed.). Pretoria: Van Schaik.

Robinson, D., Perryman, S., & Hayday, S. (2004). The drivers of employee engagement. Institute of employment studies. Brighton: Institute of employment studies.

Rousseau, D. M. (1995). Psychological Contracts in Organisations: Understanding Written and Unwritten Agreements. London: Sage Publications.

Shore, L. M., Tetrick, L. E., Taylor, M. S., Coyle-Shapiro, J., Liden, R. C., McLean Parks, J., & Van Dyne, L. (2004). The employee-organisation relationship: A timely concept in a period of transition (J. Martocchio, & G. Ferris, Eds.). Research in Personnel and Human Resources Management, 291–370.

Sisson, K. (2008, April). Putting the record straight: Industrial relations and the employment relationship (T. Colling, Ed.). Warwick papers in industrial relations(88), 1–57.

Slabbert, J. A., & Swanepoel, B. J. (2002). Introduction to Employee – Relations Management A Global Perspective (Second Edition ed.). Durban: LexisNexis.

Tsui, A. S., Pearce, J. L., Porter, L. W., & Hite, J. P. (1995). Choice of Employee-Organisation Relationship: Influence of External and Internal Organizational Factors. Research in Personnel and Human Resource Management, 13, 117–151.

van der Smissen, S., Schalk, R., & Freese, C. (2013). Contemporary psychological contracts: How both employer and employee are changing the employment relationship. Management review, 24(4), 309–327.

Webster, E. (2015). The shifting boundaries of industrial relations: Insights from South Africa. International Labour Review, 154(1), 27–36.

Webster, E. C. (1998). The politics of economic reform: Trade unions and democratization in South Africa. Journal of Contemporary African Studies, 16(1), 39–64.

Webster, E., & Buhlungu, S. (2004). Between Marginalisation & Revitalisation? The State of Trade Unionism in South Africa. Review of African Political Economy, 31(100), 229–245.

Wickens, P. D. (1995). The Ascendant Organisation. London: Macmillan Press.

Wood, G., & Coetzee, J. K. (2006). Negotiated revolutions or evolutionary regime transitions? The Czech Republic, South Africa and Chile. African Sociological Review, 10(1), 234–243.

Wright, C. F. (2011). What role for trade unions in future workplace relations? ACAS. London: ACAS. Retrieved from http://www.acas.org.uk/policydiscussion

CHAPTER 5

Engaging Unionised Employees

Abstract This chapter identifies the approaches and interventions, which may have the greatest potential to increase the engagement levels of employees in a unionised environment. The synthesis of the results shows that engaging unionised employees presents different challenges to engaging non-unionised employees. The systematic review of the literature identified strategic narrative, trust and integrity, pluralist tendencies, environmental factors, collaborative partnership, union involvement, the employment relationship, employee voice, employee participation, human resource management practices, leadership and line manager behaviour as additional antecedents that may have the greatest potential to create and embed high levels of engagement in a unionised environment. These antecedents together with the already identified antecedents informed the framework in addressing the low levels of engagement in a unionised environment.

Keywords Additional antecedents • Approaches and interventions • Engagement levels • Potential • Unionised employees

The purpose of this chapter is to identify approaches and interventions that may have the greatest potential to increase the engagement levels of employees in a unionised environment.

Although the conditions for high engagement have been studied (Kahn 1990; Maslach et al. 2001; Saks 2006; Macey and Schneider 2008; Shuck

J. H. Nel, B. Linde, *The Art of Engaging Unionised Employees*,
https://doi.org/10.1007/978-981-13-2197-9_5

et al. 2011; Harter et al. 2002), studies to determine the conditions for high engagement associated with unionised employees are lacking. Wassel (2013) is of the opinion that engagement is just as crucial in a unionised environment as in any other workplace, due to the correlation between employee engagement and overall job performance. Wassel (2013, p. 1) suggests that "companies with a unionised presence must pay special attention to engagement levels, as data suggest that unionised employees are less engaged than their non-union counterparts" are. Data gathered by Tyler (2009) corroborates Wassel's (2013) view that unionised employees are less engaged than their non-union counterparts are.

Employees often join unions in an attempt to increase satisfaction but never hit the same satisfaction levels as their non-unionised peers (Sheridan and Anderson 2013). This should not necessarily be the case, as unionised employees can also be highly engaged (Donais 2010). According to Tyler (2009), disengagement is not only a union phenomenon as it is also prevalent in both unionised and non-unionised groups (Tyler 2009).

According to Donais (2010), unionised employees, in a sense, are more engaged than non-union employees, because they are highly engaged in correcting injustices in the workplace through union activities. Their activity levels are generally higher, and their commentary about workplace systems more frequent and structured through bargaining systems (Donais 2010).

Union Worker Dissatisfaction

According to Guest and Conway (2003), the mystery of unionised worker dissatisfaction is a simple and familiar one. The primary function of unions is to promote the interests and well-being of their members; yet union members are more dissatisfied than non-union workers (Guest and Conway 2002).

To become a member of a union, employees hand their individual bargaining rights over in favour of collective bargaining rights (Donais 2010). They exchange their individual ability to negotiate with the employer for the strength of group negotiations (Donais 2010). This requires union members to take sides between their loyalty to the employer and their loyalty to the union (Donais 2010). The result is a struggle between employers and unions for the hearts and minds of employees (Donais 2010). It is it therefore not surprising that union members are less engaged than their counterparts (Donais 2010). This led to unionised employees been socialised to see a separation in interests between themselves and their employer (Donais 2010). The employee wants work that is safe and to receive fair pay and respect in the workplace. The company, on the contrary, wants to make a profit (Donais 2010).

Guest and Conway (2002) explored the paradox of union worker dissatisfaction and concluded that even after controlling a range of workplace factors trade union members remain more dissatisfied than non-union members. Guest and Conway (2002) postulate that the dissatisfaction may have something to do with being a union member. Guest and Conway (2002) identified various factors which they believe is the key reasons for union member dissatisfaction. Firstly, they identified the role of unions in raising the political awareness and the expectations of their members and the unions failure to meet these expectations. Secondly, that union members feel that their voice goes unheard in the workplace. Thirdly, that workers in high union density workplaces receive different treatment which results in a perceived anti-union stance on the part of management. Lastly, while workers join trade unions to benefit from their collective membership, there are very limited returns by way of specific outcomes or greater voice.

Chang et al. (2014) findings show that unionised employees are dissatisfied with employee involvement, health and safety, indispensability, time flexibility, workload flexibility, managerial trust and fair treatment, while non-union employees are dissatisfied with job security, pay exploitation and managerial sentiment towards unions.

The Changing Nature of Union Management Relations

A global shift in the nature of work resulted in a change in the nature and composition of the workforce (Bendix 2015). This led to the emergence of employee engagement and employee voice as forms of direct employee involvement in the late 2000s to improve organisational efficiency and productivity (Gollan and Xu 2015).

Employees have higher education levels, are more aware of their rights and are increasingly demonstrating a concern for democracy, ethical, transparent management practices, and social responsibility (Bendix 2015).

The paradox, however, is that there is still no noticeable shift in the ideological framework of business, as the free market system is still equated to capitalism (Bendix 2015) and that labour relations are more formalised and controlled through labour legislation than ever before (Salamon 1998;

Venter 2003) (as cited in Linde 2007). The employment relationship still rests on traditional pluralism and the institutionalisation of conflict, which empowers management and the unions, but leaves the employee powerless (Bendix 2015).

Gollan and Xu (2015) suggest that parties to the employment relationship should make a paradigm shift, and look beyond the adversarial relationship and embrace new models underpinned by workplace cooperation. This paradigm shift will make it possible to change the way employers and unions engage and create opportunities for employers to alter their relations with unions and employees (Yarrington et al. 2007). The replacement of the traditional industrial relations model with new management strategies, such as engagement, partnerships, collaborations, employee voice, and high-performance work organisations represent a significant change the management of employees (Yarrington et al. 2007). Engagement provides the ideal opportunity to go beyond this traditional adversarial approach (Townsend et al. 2014). Yarrington et al. (2007) regard a good union-employer relationship as one which was well established and considered ongoing.

Factors Associated with Good Union and Employer Relationships

Mainstream academics and practitioners (Kahn 1990; Maslach et al. 2001; Saks 2006; Macey and Schneider 2008; Shuck et al. 2011; Harter et al. 2002) have identified multiple antecedents for high engagement, which are illustrated in Table 3. There are, however, additional antecedents, which might also influence engagement in a unionised environment in addition to the antecedents identified by mainstream academics and practitioners. The additional antecedents, which emerged from the literature, are discussed in the next section.

Strategic Narrative

MacLeod and Clarke (2009, p. 31) defined strategic narrative as a "strong, transparent and explicit organisational culture which gives employees a line of sight between their job and the vision and aims of the organisation". MacLeod and Clarke (2009) emphasise the role of leadership in setting out this strategic narrative, ensuring that employees understand the narrative and can see how their role contributes to it.

Trust and Integrity

Dromey (2014) identified six areas of engagement drivers that will preserve employee engagement, of which trust was particularly important. Trust is a key element of the psychological contract, and Robinson et al. (2004) emphasise the similarity of engagement to the psychological contract. There has been renewed interest in the psychological contract, as with the construct of engagement since the 1990s due to various changes affecting the workplace (Guest and Conway 2002). The psychological contract can facilitate a new framework for engagement, as the traditional collective model is less relevant in many workplaces (Guest and Conway 2002). This model can accommodate the rise in individualism and flexibility and can also address the core issues of the employment relationship of trust (Guest and Conway 2002). This view is confirmed by Donais (2010), who states that trust is key for successful union engagement.

Pluralist Tendencies

The notion of employee engagement essentially comes from a unitarist perspective (Arrowsmith and Parker 2013). Unitarism refers to "employer strategies of trade union avoidance based on and justified by an ideology of a unity of interests between employers and employees, being predominantly managerial in its emphasis and application" (Fox 1974, p. 135) (as cited in Arrowsmith and Parker 2013). The contemporary notion of managerialism refers more broadly to the assertion of managerial rights, goals, and prerogatives without the need for meaningful employee involvement (Clarke and Newman 1997) (as cited in Arrowsmith and Parker 2013). This is very different from the pluralist perspective, which "sees the organisation as a coalition of interest groups" over which management presides in an authoritative but not authoritarian manner, recognising employee rights (Fox 1974, p. 10) (as cited in Arrowsmith and Parker 2013).

According to Arrowsmith and Parker (2013), engagement does not need to constitute unitarist deception to win hearts and minds in pursuit of management goals, but rather "neo-pluralist" opportunity by employers to better understanding and managing the employment relationship. The pursuit of engagement may thus combine elements of "hard" (performance-oriented) and "soft" (employee-oriented) human resource management (HRM), which we interpret as a form of "neo-pluralism" (Arrowsmith and Parker 2013).

The pluralist outlook involves a commitment to better understanding and managing the employment relationship within specific contexts, with a premium on analysis and action around employee concerns (Purcell 2012) (as cited in Arrowsmith and Parker 2013).

Environmental Factors

Hyman (1987) suggests that regardless of any management strategy, factors that are both external and internal to the organisation and the employment relationship will ensure that the strategy never completely succeeds. That many "managerial strategies" may very well be little more than tactical decision-making, rather than strategic, and that all strategies are routes to "partial failure" (1987, p. 30). Hyman (1987, p. 30) states that it is simply impossible to "harmonise the contradictions between forces and relations of production, between the production and realisation of surplus value". There is a strong body of work that identifies similar arguments to suggest that workers have faced many years of uncertainty with partially successful, but nevertheless these employees find commitment to the organisations for which they work (Edwards et al. 2001) (as cited in Townsend et al. 2014).

Delbridge and Keenoy (2010, p. 801) argue that "the practice of management can only be understood in the context of the wider social-economic, political and cultural factors which shape - if not determine - those practices". More attention must be given to organisational contextual factors, which provide both opportunities and constraints for management's ability to promote an internal context supportive of engagement efforts (Jenkins and Delbridge 2013). The prospects for delivering engaged employees are significantly influenced by the organisational approach to people management as well as how this is influenced by the complex external and internal contexts, which local management navigates (Jenkins and Delbridge 2013).

Collaborative Partnerships

Kochan (2000) (as cited in Townsend et al. 2014) argues that employees are increasingly dissatisfied with adversarial industrial relations and partnerships provide opportunities to go beyond the traditional adversarial approach. The interest in partnerships and collaboration points to an important shift from adversarial industrial relations to problem-solving outcomes among unions, managers and workers (Townsend et al. 2014).

According to Townsend et al. (2014) is a collaborative partnership where there is cooperation or collaboration for mutual gains and reciprocity between management, unions and employees. Core principles in partnerships are mutuality, dignity, respect, fairness, competitiveness, flexibility, joint and direct communication, and consultation (Townsend et al. 2014). The outcomes of collaborative partnerships can be determined through the relationships that managers, employees and unions share, employee engagement levels and reduction in turnover (Townsend et al. 2014). A sincere partnership with unions will have better results than employee engagement with a traditional adversarial approach with unions in the background (Townsend et al. 2014).

Arrowsmith and Parker (2013) suggest that human resources practioners, management must work in partnership with trade unions in pursuit of higher levels of engagement. Employers need to be committed to the partnership, as it is the key to creating relationship-driven workplaces (Arrowsmith and Parker 2013).

Union Involvement

The road to employee engagement starts with engaging the union leadership (Donais 2010). Employers must recognise that unions can help the company to increase employee engagement (Crabtree 2006). Union involvement can improve the chances of successful engagement as the unique nature of the union's relationship with employees offers many advantages for employers seeking to engage unionised employees (Donais 2010). These advantages, according to Donais (2010), are access to an established two-way communication network giving employees a "voice" which is a key component in engagement. The employer must demonstrate that it acts in the best interest of the employees by demonstrating trust and integrity, which requires involving the union (Donais 2010).

The existence of democratic union structures and operations at the enterprise level provides ordinary union members with the opportunity to participate directly in exercising worker control over their elected shop stewards, and indirectly over the policies of the union and office-bearers at the local, regional and national levels (Hirschsohn 2011). Continued union growth and maturity led to the erosion of direct democracy and increasing reliance on representative democracy through elected shop stewards (Hirschsohn 2011). It also resulted in a growing gap between workers and shop stewards and between workers and the leadership at enterprise, regional and national levels (Hirschsohn 2011). As members have disengaged from daily union activities, "ownership" and control of the union has steadily shifted from members to elected representatives and officials (Hirschsohn 2011).

It is for this reason that it is imperative to involve the unions' elected representatives and officials, because they have the power to organise their members (Donais 2010). Job satisfaction and process feedback on the success of engagement efforts can be elicited from the members by the union and will be likely to be accurate (Donais 2010). Unions will be strong advocates for the programme if they believe it will have tangible benefits for their members (Donais 2010).

The Employment Relationships

According to Kahn and Heaphy (2014), organisations are defined by sets of relationships among people who coordinate the activities in the delivery of organisational tasks and goals. Relationships affect how tasks are completed, how individuals and teams collaborate, share knowledge, and accomplish organisational objectives (Bechky 2006) (as cited in Kahn and Heaphy 2014). The relational context includes groups and teams, departments, divisions, hierarchical relations, co-workers, partnerships and peer relations (Kahn and Heaphy 2014). People join collective efforts in the context of groups and teams, because an individual's efforts become enlarged as members join together to create, discover, learn and achieve what they could not do alone (Senge 1990) (as cited in Kahn and Heaphy 2014).

According to Bendix (2015), the employment relationship will be improved by mutual interest, mutual support, trust, meaningful communication and shared goals and values. The relational context invariably shapes the extent to which people engage (Kahn and Heaphy 2014). However, only respect for individuality in the relationship can lead to personal satisfaction and meaningful relationships (Bendix 2015).

It is essential to develop sound employment relationships for workplace engagement. It is proposed that employers incorporate external influences in the development of internal employment structures. These structures should be in accordance to labour legislation and collective agreements. Furthermore, such an employment relationship should focus on the inherent requirements of the employees, to accommodate fair expectations.

These expectations should be clearly made available to the employees and made understandable, which should increase trust in the employer. Union interaction should be incorporated in the employment relationship, according to the levels of representation that it has, where similar clarity and trust could be developed.

Employee Voice

When the concept first emerged, it was associated with trade union membership and collective bargaining (Rees et al. 2013). It is now seen as referring to a broad range of ways in which employees "have a say" in the organisation through formal or informal systems of indirect, collective representation, or through direct individual channels (CIPD 2010) (as cited in Rees et al. 2013). Morrison et al. (2010) (as cited in Rees et al. 2013) refer to voice as the discretionary verbal communication of ideas, suggestions or opinions with the intent to improve organisational unit functioning.

MacLeod and Clarke (2009) identified "employee voice" alongside leadership, engaging managers and integrity as four pillars to support employee engagement. An opportunity for interaction between management and employees through broad means of communication gives employees a voice that enhances employees' propensity to engage with the organisation (Donais 2010). The opportunity for employees to have a voice in management decision-taking is fundamental in creating a positive attitude and behaviour towards the organisation. (MacLeod and Clarke 2009). MacLeod and Clarke (2009, p. 75) state that "voice becomes a building block for engagement" when 'employees' views are sought out, they are listened to and see that their opinions count and make a difference.

Rees et al. (2013) find that there is a positive connection between voice and engagement. Research done by Rees et al. (2013, p. 2) revealed that the "direct connection between the perception of voice behaviour and engagement is mediated by both employees trust in senior managers and the employee-line manager relationships".

Employee voice is more than the use of suggestion schemes, recognition and reward and getting employees to buy into corporate values, but about a two-way process where employees have an opportunity to give their views, ask questions and engage in dialogue with management (Purcell 2014). In essence, voice relates to "employees' ability to influence the outcomes of organisational decisions by having the opportunity to advance their ideas and have them considered" (Purcell 2014, p. 237). Voice should therefore be an alternative to managerial unilateralism (MacLeod and Clarke 2009).

Purcell (2014) states that good employment relations practice includes avenues for employee voice to ensure that opinions of groups affected are taken into account. Engagement can be improved through enhancing employee voice, especially in the work of employee representatives interacting with managers on strategic and policy issues (Purcell 2014). When embedded voice practices at enterprise level, led by front-line managers, co-exist with top-level consultative committees, run by senior managers, the effect is greater than on individual practices on their own (Purcell 2014). A good voice practice in a collective setting requires "a right to be informed of planned measures in advance and to have an opportunity to express an opinion prior to implementation" (Purcell 2014). This requires the establishment of a consultative committee where employee representatives, drawn from recognised trade unions or directly elected by fellow employees, or both, meet with senior managers to discuss planned business, changes, as well as issues raised by employees (Purcell 2014). Trade unions have always shown a degree of ambivalence towards consultative forums, since they prefer collective bargaining and fear that some employers will use consultative forums as a replacement for unions (Purcell 2014). According to Dromey (2014), collective voice is just as important as listening to individual employees. Understanding what the workforce as a whole is thinking is vital for employers, which generates an opportunity for trade unions to recast their relevance as the primary source of collective voice willing not just to fight for members, but to work together for the success of the business or service.

Employee Participation

Changes in the nature of work resulted in employee participation evolving since the 1980s when it was primarily a human resources management approach (Gollan and Xu 2015). The topic has had a resurgence since the global financial crisis, which not only reshaped industrial relations, but also impacts on employees (Gollan and Xu 2015). Employee participation is a form of industrial democracy, which was made possible through trade unionism and collectivism (Cressey 1995). It is aimed at direct employee involvement to improve organisational efficiency and productivity (Gollan and Xu 2015). The concept evolved further with employee empowerment gaining prominence in the 1990s, high commitment and performance took over in the early 2000s, and employee engagement in the 2010s (Wilkinson et al. 2010). Gollan and Xu (2015) state that the major shifts in employee participation reflect the major shifts that took place since the 1980s in the industrial relations landscape. According to Knudsen et al. (2011) is the rationale behind participation industrial democracy, social integration and organisational efficiency. According to Anstey (1997a), employee participation is a great motivational tool, because it gives people a degree of control, and provides scope for personal growth (Anstey 1997a). These are in themselves intrinsic rewards, which flow from the performance of a job within a participatory environment (Anstey 1997a).

Terms like participation, engagement and involvement are at times used interchangeably, whereas the meanings and forms that the term "employee participation" can take vary across disciplines (Wilkinson et al. 2010). Knudsen et al. (2011, p. 384) state that employee participation essentially encompasses "all forms through which employees take part in decisions regarding their job and their workplace". "Forms of employee participation can be direct or indirect, formal or informal workplace arrangements" (Knudsen et al. 2011, p. 384). "These various forms of participation differ in the scope of decision making, the degree of influence workers have over management, and the organisational level at which decisions are made" (Gollan and Xu 2015, p. 4). Some forms of participation give employee a voice, which may range from a modest role in decision-making to employee involvement in organisational governance (Gollan and Xu 2015). The spectrum of participation is determined by each form of participation's depth as well as its scope (Knudsen et al. 2011). The depth may vary from the mere information sharing with management, to consultation and joint talks and negotiations, to self-determination (Knudsen et al. 2011). The scope of participation according to Knudsen et al. (2011, p. 384) stretches "from operational matters (related to the job/task), through tactical matters (related to work organization, technology and pay systems, etc.), to strategic issues (related to company missions and goals, investment and de-investment, etc.)". The worker participation model that gives unions the most influence at enterprise level in the west is probably the co-determination and works council system in Germany (Anstey 1997a).

Institutionalised participation takes strategic engagement some steps further, because it provides a stronger form of stakeholder rights in the company than strategic engagement does (Anstey 1997a). It can be seen as a way of transforming the workplace by extending democracy and citizenship rights into it (Anstey 1997a).

The characteristics and outcomes related to employee participation can be contingent on many contextual factors, such as regulatory condition, sector, industrial relations climate, organisational and employee characteristics, motives of actors, employer control and union strength (Gollan and Xu 2015).

Human Resources Management Practices

Organisations must move beyond the routine management of annual engagement surveys and must entrench engagement in all human resource management (HRM) practices (Albrecht et al. 2015). HRM practices focused on engagement directly influence the psychological experiences of safety, meaningfulness and availability at work, and can facilitate and improve employee engagement (Albrecht et al. 2015). In order for engagement to deliver its claimed benefits, it needs to be explicitly embedded within an integrated system of HRM policies, practices and procedures (Guest 2014a). Bowen and Ostroff (2004) (cited in Truss et al. 2013) suggested that employee engagement might finally provide the key to understanding how effective HRM practice may lead to higher individual and organisational performance.

The concern with linking HRM and performance has, however, been challenged for its unitarist view of organisational life (Delbridge and Keenoy 2010). Arrowsmith and Parker (2013) argue that the pursuit of higher engagement levels may represent a "neo-pluralist" turn in the values and practices of human resources management (Arrowsmith and Parker 2013). This involves much more than simply offering transactional human resources related services to management in pursuit of a "unitarist" agenda, even if the process is largely based around mutual gains. It offers an opportunity to reconcile "soft" (employee-centred) human resources practices to "hard" (performance-orientated) goals (Arrowsmith and Parker 2013). Efforts to foster high levels of engagement can be driven either from a will to gain competitive advantage ("hard" engagement) or, conversely, from a desire to improve working conditions and the employment relationship ("soft" engagement) (Truss et al. 2013).

Albrecht et al. (2015) emphasised that engagement needs to be integrated as a focus across all facets of the employer-employee relationship.

This means that engagement needs to be strategically embedded and supported across the total human resources value chain. This offers HRM the opportunity to systematically engage with its core constituencies in the pursuit of a clear contribution to workplace motivation and performance (Arrowsmith and Parker 2013).

Leadership and Line Manager Behaviour

Alfes et al. (2013) found that employees' perceptions of line manager behaviour are positively related to levels of employee engagement. Rees et al. (2013, p. 2780) also found that there is a "direct connection between perceptions of voice behaviour and engagement is mediated by both employees trust in senior management and the employee-line manager relationship".

Northouse (2001) in Dhivya and Sripirabaa (2015, p. 140) defines leadership as "a process whereby one individual influences a group of individuals to achieve a common goal". Dhivya and Sripirabaa (2015) place leadership into various categories of which leader member exchange (LMX) is one. According to them, the LMX process is unique as it refers to the quality of the relationship between the parties. High-quality LMX relationships are categorised by a high degree of interaction, support and trust (Crawford et al. 2014). Xanthopoulou et al. (2009), Christian et al. (2011) all established that there is a positive relationship between LMX and engagement levels.

The interaction between managers and employees represents a significant source of engagement (Soane et al. 2012). However, the role of leaders must be seen within the job context as work roles are the channel for engagement (Soane et al. 2012).

The JD-R model is a useful conceptual model for understanding how a job resource, such as supportive leadership, may relate to employee engagement (Bakker and Demerouti 2007). The first premise of the JD-R model is that in every job there are certain job demands and job resources (Schaufeli 2013). Job demands are "physical, psychological, social, or organizational aspects of a job that require sustained physical and/or psychological (cognitive or emotional) effort or skills" and are therefore associated with physiological and psychological costs (Bakker and Demerouti 2007, p. 312). Two recent studies according to Baxter (2013) lend support to leadership as a job resource and how it fits into the JD-R model.

High-Performance Work Organisations and Environments

The effectiveness of high-involvement work practices on engagement levels and positive organisational outcomes are well documented (Konrad 2006). Employees who are involved in conceiving, designing and implementing workplace and process changes are engaged employees (Konrad 2006). High-performance work organisations (HPWO) practices can develop the positive beliefs and attitudes associated with employee engagement, and these practices can generate discretionary behaviours that can lead to enhanced performance (Konrad 2006).

Kirkman et al. (1999, p. 8) define HPWO as "an organisational system that continually aligns its strategy, goals, objectives, and internal operations with the demands of its external environment to maximise organisational performance". The notion behind the concept of the HPWO is that it can deliver reasonable advantage because it enables firms to deliver increased performance because of socially consensual management practices (Stewart and Danford 2008). Inherent to socially consensual management practices include the linking of organisational goals mediated by partnership arrangements, whether formal or informal (Stewart and Danford 2008).

Lawler (2001) identified four interlocking principles for building an HPWO work system to ensure its effectiveness and that the various principles will work in synergy to ensure high engagement levels. These components are to provide employees with the power to make decisions, information about the business, knowledge of work and rewards tied to business results (Kirkman et al. 1999).

Lawler (2001) suggests that the implementation of HPWO environment requires that every major feature of the organisation needs to be re-designed. This requires the participation of all employees in the re-design of the organisation. This degree of participation generates a positive attitude amongst all employees towards a change in high involvement (Konrad 2006). Kirkman et al. (1999) are of the opinion that HPWOs utilise five components to various degrees to dynamically adjust to its environment. These components are self-managing work teams; employee involvement, participation, empowerment; total quality management; integrated production technologies and the learning organisation (Kirkman et al. 1999).

The key concepts and themes that emerged from the literature review on the approaches and interventions that may have the greatest potential to increase the engagement levels of employees in a unionised context were organised around key antecedents. These newly discovered antecedents that will inform the framework are summarised in Table 5.1.

Table 5.1 Antecedents associated with high levels of engagement in a unionised environment

Article citation/Author	*Antecedents*
Albrecht et al. (2015)	Human Resources Management Practices
Gollan and Xu (2015)	Employee participation
Knudsen et al. (2011)	
Arrowsmith and Parker (2013)	Pluralist tendencies
Chang et al. (2014)	Job security
	Managerial sentiment towards unions
	Fair pay "non-pay exploitation"
Townsend et al. (2014)	Collaborative partnership
	Managerial strategies
Purcell (2014)	Employee voice
Rees et al. (2013)	
Dundon et al. (2004)	
Alfes et al. (2013)	Line manager behaviour
	Human Resource Management practices
Jenkins and Delbridge (2013)	Labour relations system and context
Hirschsohn (2011)	Trade union democracy
Donais (2010)	Union involvement
	Communication giving employees a voice
	Safety
	Fair pay
	Respect
	Trust and integrity
	Involving union representatives
Francis et al. (2013)	Conversational practices
MacLeod and Clarke (2009)	Strategic narrative
	Engaging managers
	Employee voice
	Integrity
Stewart and Danford (2008)	Union involvement
Shuck and Albornoz (2008)	Opportunity to learn
Soane et al. (2012)	Management practices
Yarrington et al. (2007)	Trust
	Communication
	Employee voice
	Respect for rules of the relationship
	Individual professional credibility
	Role of managers
	Pluralist tendencies
	Line manager dynamics
Konrad (2006)	High-performance work organisation and environment
Holbeche and Springett (2003)	Meaning

(*continued*)

Table 5.1 (continued)

Article citation/Author	*Antecedents*
Guest and Conway (2002)	Voice Individual Collective Meeting expectations created by members Equal opportunities Trust
Hyman (1987)	External and internal factors to the organisation
Salamon (1998)	Micro and macro environment
Linde (2007) Shore et al. (2004) Bendix (2015) Finnemore (2009) Anstey (1997a) Rousseau (1995)	Employee organisation relationship Psychological contract Employment relationship
Finnemore (2009) Slabbert and Myburgh (2000) Slabbert and Swanepoel (2002) Anstey (1997a, b) Adler (1998) Webster and Von Holdt (2005) Buhlungu and Tshoaedi (2012)	The labour relations system

References

Adler, G. (1998). Engaging the State and Capital: Labour and the Deepening of Democracy in South Africa. Law Democracy and Development, 2(17), 1–26.

Albrecht, S. L., Bakker, A. B., Gruman, J. A., Macey, W. A., & Saks, A. M. (2015). Employee engagement, human resources management practices and competitive advantage: An integrated approach. Journal of Organisational Effectiveness: People and Performance, 2(1), 7–35.

Alfes, K., Truss, C., Soane, E. C., Rees, C., & Gatenby, M. (2013, November–December). The relationship between line manager behavior, perceived HRM practices, and individual performance: Examining the mediating role of engagement. Human Resources Management, 52(6), 839–859.

Anstey, M. (1997a). Employee Participation and workplace forums. Kenwyn: Juta & Co, Ltd.

Anstey, M. (1997b). Labour Relations in Transition: A changing South Africa in a changing world. Port Elizabeth: Mark Anstey.

Arrowsmith, J., & Parker, J. (2013). The meaning of 'employee engagement' for the values and roles of the HRM function. The international journal of Human Resource management, 24(14), 2692–2717.

Bakker, A. B., & Demerouti, E. (2007). The Job Demands-Resources model: stat of the art. Journal of Managerial Psychology, 22(3), 309–328.

Bakker, A. B., Demerouti, E., Taris, T. W., Schaufeli, W. B., Schreurs, P. J. G. (2003) A multigroup analysis of the job demands-resources model in four home care organizations. International Journal of Stress Management, 10 (1):16–38.

Bendix, S. (2015). Labour relations: A southern African perspective (Sixth edition ed.). Cape Town: Juta.

Buhlungu, S., & Tshoaedi, M. (2012). Cosatu's Contested Legacy (First ed.). Cape Town: HSRC Press.

Baxter, L. E. (2013). Supportive Leadership, Employee Engagement and Occupational Safety: A Field Study. PhD Dissertation. Knoxville, Tennessee: University of Tennessee.

Chang, J., Travaglione, A., & O'Neill, G. (2014). Analyzing job attitudes between unionized and non-unionized. 2014 Cambridge Conference Business & Economics (pp. 1–21). Cambridge: ABER.

Christian, M. S., Garza, A. S., & Slaughter, J. E. (2011). Work engagement: A qualitative review and test of its relations with task and contextual performance. Personnel Psychology, 64, 89–136.

Crabtree, S. (2006, May). Can Managers Engage Unionized Employees? The Gallup Management Journal. Retrieved from http://www.gmj.gallup.com

Crawford, E. R., Rich, B. L., Buckman, B., & Bergeron, J. (2014). The antecedents and drivers of employee engagement. In C. Truss, R. Delbridge, K. Alfes, A. Shantz, & E. Soane, Employee engagement in theory and practice (pp. 57–81). New York: Routledge.

Cressey, P. (1995, March). Extended Review: Employee Participation. Work, Employment & Society, 9(1), 187–190.

Delbridge, R., & Keenoy, T. (2010). Beyond managerialism? The International Journal of Human Resource Management, 21(6), 799–817.

Dhivya, A. S., & Sripirabaa, B. (2015). The impact of leader member exchange on work engagement: an empirical study. International Journal of Management, 6(1), 139–150.

Donais, Blaine. (2010). Engaging unionised employees: Employee morale and productivity. Ontario, Canada: Thomson Reuters.

Dromey, J. (2014). MacLeod and Clarke's concept of employee engagement: An analysis based on the workplace employment relations study. Acas. London: Acas.

Dundon, T., Wilkinson, A., Marchington, M., & Ackers, P. (2004). The meanings and purpose of employee voice. The International Journal of Human Resource Management, 15(6), 1149–1170.

Finnemore, M. (2009). Introduction to labour relations in South Africa (Tenth Edition ed.). Durban: LexisNexis.
Fox, A. (1974). Man Mismanagement. London: Hutchinson.
Francis, H. M., Ramdhony, A., Reddington, M., Staines, H. (2013) Opening spaces for conversational practice: a conduit for effective engagement strategies and productive working arrangements. The International Journal of Human Resource Management 24, (14), 2713–2740.
Gollan, P. J., & Xu, J. (2015). Re-engagement with the employee participation debate: beyond the case of contested and captured terrain. Work, employment and society, 29(2), 1–13.
Guest, D. (2014a). Employee engagement: A sceptical analysis. Journal of Organizational Effectiveness: People and Performance, 1(2), 141–156.
Guest, D. E. (2014b). Employee engagement: Fashionable fad or long-term fixture? In C. Truss, R. Delbridge, K. Alfes, A. Shantz, & E. Soane, Employee engagement in theory and practice (pp. 221–235). London: Routledge.
Guest, D. E., & Conway, N. (2002). Pressure at work and the psychological contract. London: CIPD.
Guest, D., & Conway, N. (2003). Exploring the paradox of union worker dissatisfaction. King's College, University of London, Human resource management and employment relations. London: King's College, University of London.
Harter, J. K., Schmidt, F. L., & Hayes, T. L. (2002). Business-unit-level relationship between employee satisfaction, employee engagement, and business outcomes: A meta-analysis. Journal of Applied Psychology, 87(2), 268–279.
Hirschsohn, P. (2011). The "hollowing-out" of trade union democracy in Cosatu? Members, shop stewards and the South African Communist Party. Law Democracy & Development, 15, 279–310.
Holbeche, L., & Springett, N. (2003). In Search of Meaning in the Workplace. Horsham: Roffey Park.
Hyman, R. (1987). Strategy or structure? Capital, labour and control. Work, employment and Society, 1, 25–55.
Jenkins, S., & Delbridge, R. (2013). Context matters: examining 'soft' and 'hard' approaches to employee engagement in two workplaces. The International Journal of Human Resource Management, 24(14), 2670–2691.
Kahn, W. A. (1990). Psychological conditions of personal engagement and disengagement at work. Academy of Management Journal, 33(4), 692–724.
Kahn, W. A., & Heaphy, E. D. (2014). Relational context of personal engagement at work. In C. Truss, R. Delbridge, K. Alfes, A. Shantz, & E. Soane, Employee engagement in theory and practice (pp. 83–96). London: Routledge.
Kirkman, B. L., Lowe, K. B., & Young, D. P. (1999). High-performance work organizations: definitions, practices, and an annotated bibliography. Greensboro, North Carolina: CCL Press.
Knudsen, H., Busck, O., & Lind, J. (2011). Work environment quality: The role of workplace participation and democracy. Work Employment and Society, 25(3), 379–396.

Konrad, A. M. (2006, March/April). Ivey business journal. Retrieved from http://iveybusinessjournal.com/publication/engaging-employees-through-high-involvement-work-practices/

Lawler, E. E. (2001). Designing high performance organisations. Columbia: University of Southern California. Retrieved from http://unpan1.un.org/intradoc/groups/public/documents/un/unpan001316~1.pdf

Linde, B. J. (2007). Employment Relations, the psychological contract and work wellness in the Higher Education Sector in South Africa. Ridderkerk, Netherlands: Ridderprint B.V.

Macey, W., & Schneider, B. (2008). The Meaning of Employee Engagement. Industrial and Organizational Psychology, 3–30.

MacLeod, D., & Clarke, N. (2009). Engaging for success: Enhancing performance through employee engagement. Department for Business, Innovation and Skills. London: A report to Government.

Maslach, C., Schaufeli, W. B., & Leiter, M. P. (2001). Job burnout. Annual Review of Psychology, 52, 397–422.

Purcell, J. (2014). Employee voice and engagement. In C. Truss, R. Delbridge, K. Alfes, A. Shantz, & E. Soane, Employee engagement in theory and practice (pp. 236–249). London: Routledge.

Rees, C., Alfes, K., & Gatenby, M. (2013). Employee voice and engagement: Connections and consequences. International Journal of Human Resource Management, 24(14), 2780–2798.

Robinson, D., Perryman, S., & Hayday, S. (2004). The drivers of employee engagement. Institute of employment studies. Brighton: Institute of employment studies.

Rousseau, D. M. (1995). Psychological Contracts in Organisations: Understanding Written and Unwritten Agreements. London: Sage Publications.

Saks, A. M. (2006). Antecedents and consequences of employee engagement. Journal of Managerial Psychology, 21(7), 600–619.

Salamon, M. (1998). Industrial Relations: Theory and practice (3rd ed.). Hertfordshire, United Kingdom: Prentice Hall.

Schaufeli, W. (2013). Employee Engagement in Theory and Practice (C. Truss, K. Alfes, R. Delbridge, A. Shantz, & E. Soane, Eds.). London: Routledge.

Sheridan, K., & Anderson, K. (2013, July 24). HR Solutions eNews. Retrieved July 24, 2013, from http://avatarsolutions.com/resources/enews-0311/Unionized-0311.html

Shore, L. M., Tetrick, L. E., Taylor, M. S., Coyle-Shapiro, J., Liden, R. C., McLean Parks, J., & Van Dyne, L. (2004). The employee-organisation relationship: A timely concept in a period of transition. (J. Martocchio, & G. Ferris, Eds.) Research in Personnel and Human Resources Management, 291–370.

Shuck, B., & Albornoz, C. (2008). Exploring employee engagement among three non-salaried employees: A phenomenological study. In M. S. Plakhotnik & S. M. Nielsen (Eds.), Proceedings of the Seventh Annual College of Education

Research Conference: Urban and International Section (pp. 138–143). Miami: Florida International University. http://coeweb.fiu.edu/research_conference/.
Shuck, B., Rocco, T. S., & Reio, T. G. (2011). Employee Engagement: an examination of antecedent and outcome variables. Human Resources Development International, 14(4), 428–446.
Slabbert, J. A., & Myburgh, P. A. (2000). The psycho-social contract as departure point for managing by values. In J. A. Slabbert, J. J. Prinsloo, B. J. Swanepoel, W. Backer, & L. Taylor (Ed.), Managing emploment relations in South Afirca (pp. 19-1–19-32). Durban: Butterworth Publishers (Pty) Ltd.
Slabbert, J. A., & Swanepoel, B. J. (2002). Introduction to Employee – Relations Management A Global Perspective (Second Edition ed.). Durban: LexisNexis.
Soane, E., Truss, K., Alfes, K., Shantz, A., Rees, C., & Gatenby, M. (2012). Development and application of a new measure of employee engagement: the ISA engagement scale. Human resource development international, 15(5), 529–547.
Stewart, P., & Danford, A. (2008). Editorial: Union Strategies and Worker Engagement with New Forms of Work and Employment. New Technology, Work and Employment, 23(3), 146–150.
Townsend, K., Wilkinson, A., & Burgess, J. (2014). Routes to partial success: collaborative employment relations and employee engagement. The International Journal of Human Resources Management, 25(6), 915–930.
Truss, C., Shantz, A., Soane, E., Alfes, K., & Delbridge, R. (2013). Employee engagement, organisational performance and individual well-being: Exploring the evidence, developing the theory. The International Journal of Human Resources Management, 24(14), 2657–2669.
Tyler, J. (2009). Employee Engagement and Labour Relations. Retrieved May 31, 2013, from businessjournal.gallup.com: http://businessjournal.gallup.com
Wassel, C. (2013). www.hrsolutionsinc.com. Retrieved May 31, 2013, from HR Solutions, Inc.
Webster, E., & Von Holdt, K. (2005). Beyond the Apartheid Workplace: Studies in Transition. Scottsville: University of KwaZulu-Natal Press.
Wilkinson, A., Gollan, P. J., Marchington, M., & Lewin, D. (2010). Conceptualizing employee participation in organisations. In A. Wilkinson, P. J. Gollan, M. Marchington, D. Lewin, A. Wilkinson, P. J. Gollan, M. Marchington, & D. Lewin (Eds.), The Oxford Handbook of Participation in Organisations (pp. 3–25). Oxford: Oxford University Press.
Xanthopoulou, D., Bakker, A., Demerouti, E., & Schaufeli, W. (2009). Work engagement and financial returns: A diary study on the role o f job and personal resources. Journal of Occupational and Organizational Psychology (82), 183–200.
Yarrington, L., Townsend, K., & Brown, K. (2007). Models of Engagement: Union Management Relations for the 21st Century. AIRAANZ Conference 7–9 February 2007, University of Auckland New Zealand. Auckland: Queensland University of Technology.

CHAPTER 6

Framework for Engaging Unionised Employees

Abstract This chapter presents the findings of the systematic review of the literature to produce a narrative around the evidence in order to bring into focus suitable propositions to develop a framework to address the low levels of engagement in a unionised environment. The evidence relating to the antecedents within the general workforce and the newly discovered antecedents associated with high levels of employee engagement in a unionised environment, were synthesised to determine the elements to be included in the overall framework. Eleven propositions emerged from the evidence synthesis which has been used to create the conceptual framework. The framework illustrates how job design factors, trust and integrity, individual characteristics, collaborative partnerships, voice, HRM practices, leadership and line managers' behaviour and individual characteristics influence engagement.

Keywords Findings • Framework • Levels of engagement • Propositions • Synthesis

Findings

The aim of this evidence synthesis is to systematically analyse themes in the literature to produce a critical narrative around the evidence in order to bring into focus suitable propositions to develop a framework to address the low levels of engagement in a unionised environment. The approach

J. H. Nel, B. Linde, *The Art of Engaging Unionised Employees*,
https://doi.org/10.1007/978-981-13-2197-9_6

to the evidence synthesis was founded on the recommendations of Briner and Denyer (2012), for conducting a systematic review using a narrative approach that adhered to the principles of quality, relevance, transparency, replicability and credibility. The evidence synthesis was guided by the following five questions.

How Has Engagement Been Defined and Conceptualised Within the Academic and Practitioner Literature?

The purpose of addressing this question was to identify suitable concepts, frameworks and practices to develop a theoretical framework in a unionised environment. Data from 103 sources was extracted and 48 sources were included in the evidence synthesis to determine how to increase the engagement levels of employees in a unionised environment.

In the analysis of the literature, seven predominant definitions of engagement were identified; three of these definitions have been operationalised in six engagement scales.

Kahn's (1990) personal engagement definition views engagement as people employing and expressing themselves physically, cognitively, emotionally and mentally during role performance. His definition has been operationalised in the form of quantitate personal engagement scales developed by May et al. (2004), Rich et al. (2010) and Soane et al. (2012).

The second stream of research views engagement as a positive effective-motivational state of mind directed towards work tasks (Maslach et al. 2001). Work task engagement is founded on the notion that engagement is on the positive end of the burnout antithesis (Schaufeli 2013). Building on the notion of work task engagement, the "Utrecht Group" developed the Utrecht Work Engagement Scale (UWES) that consists of 17 items measuring the vigour, dedication and absorption dimensions (Schaufeli and Bakker 2004).

The multidimensional approach emerged from a multidimensional perspective of employee engagement conceptualised by Saks (2006, p. 602), who defined the multidimensional concept of engagement as "a distinct and unique construct that consists of cognitive, emotional, and behavioural components that are associated with individual role performance". Saks (2006) developed a six-item scale to measure job engagement and a six-item scale to measure organisational engagement.

Stumpf et al. (2013) developed a two-dimensional measure of engagement for professionals in technically orientated workgroups that measure felt engagement and behavioural engagement. It examines the relationship of engagement to five workgroup outcomes namely, innovation, performance, satisfaction with the organisation, career success and intention to stay.

Shuck and Wollard (2010) conducted a historical analysis of engagement and they identified several inconsistencies and consistencies from the various definitions. The two main inconsistencies are a lack of clarity about where the decision to become engaged develops and the types of engagement (Shuck and Wollard 2010). Kahn's (1990) original theory of engagement focused on the employee being able to express him/herself at work and became vague over time towards a more organisationally cantered term (Welbourne and Schlachter 2014).

A wide range of theoretical frameworks has been used to define the state of engagement of which the needs-satisfying approach conceptualised by Kahn (1990) still provides the strongest theoretical rationale for understanding the psychology of engagement, compared to any other model. Kahn (1990) has been clear about the psychological conditions that lead to engagement as well as the factors that influence each of the psychological conditions, compared to other constructs (Saks and Gruman 2014).

According to Bailey et al. (2015), the foremost theoretical framework used to define engagement as a psychological state is the JD-R framework. The JD-R framework distinguishes between resources and is based on the view that both job and personal resources serve to energise people and foster high engagement levels and that high job demands sparks a health impairment process that inhibits engagement (Schaufeli 2013).

The second most widespread theory used in the literature is SET, which is based on norms of reciprocity (Bailey et al. 2015). It is argued that employees with positive perceptions of how their employer views them would be more likely to respond by investing personal effort into their work in the form of raised levels of engagement (Alfes et al. 2013).

This process revealed the complexity and indistinctness within the academic literature relating to the definition, meaning, modelling and operationalisation of engagement (Schaufeli 2013).

What Do Academics and Practitioners Recognise as Conditions (Antecedents) for High Levels of Engagement (Outcomes)?

The purpose of addressing this question was to identify the antecedents and outcomes of engagement that has already been researched and validated and that will have the greatest potential to increase the levels of engagement in a unionised environment. This process identified a number of strategies or conditions that precede the development of engagement as well as the individual and organisational benefits of engagement.

Data from 24 sources was extracted and 7 sources were included in the evidence synthesis to answer this question. No academic literature addressing the antecedents and consequences of engagement in a unionised environment was discovered during the search.

The synthesis of the results showed that engagement is considered a mediating variable in which antecedents influence engagement levels and engagement in turn leads to individual and organisational outcomes (Saks and Gruman 2014). A number of individual and organisational antecedents have emerged from the synthesis that point towards approaches that influence engagement levels. Bailey et al. (2015) conducted a comprehensive narrative synthesis on the antecedents and outcomes of engagement and found that job resources, individual psychological states, positive perceptions of leadership and line management, as well as a positive perception of the organisation and team has a "similarly strong impact" on engagement which will guide the final framework. The literature suggests that negative antecedents such as dysfunctional leadership, poor communication, continuous quality improvement efforts, defiant behaviour, hindrance demand, bullying, adherence to co-worker norms, self-consciousness and abusive supervision are associated with lower levels of engagement (Bailey et al. 2015; Crawford et al. 2014)

The outcomes of engagement were examined under two main headings, namely individual performance related outcomes and organisational related outcomes. The outcomes were classified under the same headings for the purposes of the conceptual framework. The synthesis of the evidence on individual outcomes revealed that engagement was most strongly correlated with job satisfaction and organisational commitment, in-role and extra-role performance, life satisfaction and general health (Bailey et al. 2015). The synthesis of the evidence on organisational outcomes revealed that engagement was most strongly correlated with customer satisfaction, turnover intention, safety, productivity and profitability (Gupta and Sharma 2016).

The synthesis of the literature revealed that the literature is mostly silent on the negative consequences of high engagement levels. The literature search on the negative consequences of engagement revealed mostly comments and articles relating to this topic. The most significant comments were from George (2011), Halbesleben (2011) and Truss et al. (2013), in which George (2011) and Halbesleben (2011) were of the opinion that high engagement levels might not necessarily be a constructive experience for employees.

What Circumstances Influence Engagement Levels in a Unionised Environment?

The third question addressed the relationship between employees and organisations, as well as the impact of environmental factors on engagement levels in a unionised environment. Data from 140 sources was extracted and 49 sources were included in the evidence synthesis to answer this question.

The evidence indicates that the EOR is an overarching term describing the relationship between the employee and the organisation and that it includes the concepts of employee engagement, psychological empowerment and the psychological contract (Coyle-Shapiro and Shore 2007). Although the "psychological contract and psychological empowerment could be considered a pattern of the EOR they do not exhibit a high level of employee activation and mutual exchange relationship simultaneously" in a connected manner (Eldor and Vigoda-Gadot 2016, p. 10). This holistic pattern is, however, evident in engagement, and engagement may provide a better explanation of the contemporary EOR (Eldor and Vigoda-Gadot 2016). Employee engagement has the potential to redefine the optimal EOR (Eldor and Vigoda-Gadot 2016, p. 20).

Evidence suggests that the SET provides the theoretical foundation for understanding the EOR and that it seems closely related to other constructs, including employee engagement (Hall 2015). Evidence further suggests that there are various related points between engagement and the psychological contract, in that both are unwritten, reinforced by trust, and are reciprocal relationships that can be violated (Robinson et al. 2004).

The employment relationship, as part of the EOR, is the primary exchange relationship between the individual employee and employer (Shore et al. 2004). It is a complex relationship because it simultaneously features elements of conflict and commonality of interest (Nel et al. 2016). At the heart of this relationship are the employee, trade unions, employment regulations and the psychological contract (Shore et al. 2004). The employment relationship is key to the functioning of the broader labour relations system, which consists out of the various actors within the constraints of various environmental influences (Finnemore 2009). The inherent characteristics of the employment relationship is a desire by the actors to manage the relationship by means of employment regulations that manifest themselves in legislations, policies, procedures and codes (Linde 2007).

The evidence suggests that despite literature examining different approaches to managing the employment relationship, debate exists about the means to provide fair, just and profitable workplaces due to the "contested terrain" (Edwards 1979) (as cited in Townsend). Hyman (1987) suggests that the contradictory objectives of consent and control in the employment relationship operating within unpredictable external environments means that there is no single best way of managing the EOR. Contextual "factors that are both external and internal to the organisation and the employment relationship will ensure that the strategy never completely succeeds and that many 'managerial strategies' may very well be little more than tactical decision-making, rather than strategic" (Hyman 1987, p. 29).

The synthesis of the evidence indicated that this complexity is driven by a number of economic, legal, market, structural, technological, social and individual changes, which occurred since the late 1980s in many countries. These factors fundamentally affected the nature of work, organisations, the workforce and the shape of modern business (Wood and Coetzee 2006).

These factors and the unions' response to it affect an employer's choice of forms of EOR focussing on employability and flexibility (Tsui et al. 1995). These factors, according to Tsui et al. (1995), shed light on the paradox that organisations need to manage. This paradox, according to Tsui et al. (1995), stems from the fact that organisations simultaneously depend more on their employees, ask more from them, while offering less in return. The challenge for organisations is to "balance" these factors, as they influence how organisations relate to their employees to drive engagement (Tsui et al. 1995).

What Approaches and Interventions Have the Greatest Potential to Create and Embed High Levels of Engagement in a Unionised Environment?

The purpose of the fourth question was to identify antecedents in addition to the antecedents already researched and validated that have the greatest potential to increase the engagement levels of employees in a unionised environment.

Data from 99 sources was extracted and 29 sources were included in the evidence synthesis to answer this question.

Data gathered showed that unionised employees are less engaged than their non-union counterparts and that employees often join unions in an attempt to increase satisfaction, but never hit the same satisfaction levels as their non-unionised peers (Sheridan and Anderson 2013; Tyler 2009;

Wassel 2013). The synthesis of the results shows that there are significant differences between union and non-union employees, and that engaging unionised employees presents different challenges to engaging non-unionised employees. Although it is commonly accepted that unionised employees are less engaged than their non-union counterparts, the synthesis of the results shows that studies to determine the conditions for high engagement associated with unionised employees are non-existent. In line with the question to identify what approaches and interventions have the greatest potential to increase the engagement levels of employees in a unionised environment, the synthesis identified several antecedents that are specifically associated with high levels of engagement in a unionised environment, as illustrated in Table 5.1.

The additional antecedents identified are strategic narrative, trust and integrity, pluralist tendencies, environmental factors, collaborative partnership, union involvement, the employment relationship, employee voice, employee participation, HRM practices, leadership and line manager's behaviour and HPWO. These antecedents, together with the job resources, individual psychological states, positive perceptions of leadership and line management, as well as a positive perception of the organisation will be combined into several propositions for the development of the framework.

What Could a Framework for Engagement in a Unionised Context Look Like in Order to Increase Engagement Levels?

The purpose of addressing this question was to develop a framework to address the low levels of engagement in a unionised environment based on the evidence discovered during the systematic review of the literature.

Data from 16 sources was extracted and 1 source was included in the evidence synthesis to identify the antecedents that have demonstrated to have the biggest potential to increase the engagement levels of employees in a unionised environment. There is disappointingly not much academic research on this topic and the only source included was from practitioners' literature.

The evidence relating to the individual and organisational antecedents within the general workforce (prevailing antecedents) and the antecedents associated with high levels of employee engagement in a unionised environment (additional antecedents), were synthesised to determine the elements to be included in the overall framework. The prevailing antecedents and the additional antecedents are illustrated in Table 6.1.

Table 6.1 Prevailing antecedents and additional antecedents discovered associated with high levels of engagement in a unionised environment

Prevailing antecedents	*Additional antecedents*
Job challenge	Human Resources Management practices
Autonomy	Employee participation
Variety	Pluralist tendencies
Feedback	Job security
Fit	Managerial sentiment towards unions
Opportunities for development	Fair pay "non-pay exploitation"
Reward and recognition	Collaborative partnership
Social support	Managerial strategies
Transformational leadership	Line manager behaviour
Leader-member exchange	Labour relations system and context
Workplace climate	Trade union democracy
Organisational justice	Communication giving employees a voice
Job security	Safety
Role overload	Respect
Work-role conflict	Trust and integrity
Family-work conflict	Involving union representatives
Resource inadequacies	Conversational practices
Time urgency	Strategic narrative
Off-work recovery	Engaging managers
Disposition	Union involvement
Personal resources	Opportunity to learn
Sustainable workload	Management practices
Feelings of choice and control	Employee voice
Recognition and reward	Respect for rules of the relationship
Supportive work community	Individual professional credibility
Fairness and justice	Role of managers
Meaningful and valued work	Pluralist tendencies
Meaning	Line manager dynamics
Job enrichment	High-performance work organisation
Work-role fit	Meaning
Rewarding co-workers	Voice
Supportive supervisor	Individual
Resources	Collective
Social exchange involving reciprocity	Meeting expectations created by members
Individual differences	Equal opportunities
Job resources and personal resources	Trust
Have the capacity to engage	External and internal factors to the organisation
Have a reason or motivation to engage	Micro and macro environment
Have the freedom to engage	Employee— organisation relationship
Know how to engage	Psychological contract
	Employment relationship
	The labour relations system

Table 6.2 Outcomes associated with high levels of engagement in a unionised environment

Organisational outcomes	*Individual outcomes*
Customer Satisfaction	Job satisfaction
Turnover intention	Organisational commitment
Safety	In-role performance
Productivity	Job performance
Profitability	Extra-role performance
	Organisational citizenship behaviour
	Innovation
	Life satisfaction
	General health

The evidence relating to the individual and organisational outcomes associated with high levels of employee engagement in a unionised environment were also synthesised to determine the elements to be included in the overall framework. These outcomes are illustrated in Table 6.2 below.

The conceptual framework, which is discussed in detail in the next section, illustrates a pathway, linking the antecedents to employee engagement and performance outcomes which were discovered during the synthesis of the evidence.

Propositions of a Conceptual Framework of Engagement

After systematically analysing the literature on engagement, 11 propositions emerged from the evidence synthesis that will increase the engagement levels in a unionised environment. These propositions are the following:

1. That individual characteristics shape people's predispositions towards engagement or disengagement and are antecedents to engagement (Kahn 1990). The systematic review of the literature suggests that individual psychological states like experiencing meaningfulness, safety and availability could be antecedents to

engagement. The synthesis of the literature revealed that individual characteristics like, a proactive personality, optimism, conscientiousness, trait and self-efficacy are prominent antecedents of engagement (Bailey et al. 2015; Christian et al. 2011; Wollard and Shuck 2011).

2. That a key component of employee engagement is integrity and trust. Despite its importance, organisations experience a decline in the levels of employee trust towards managers (Davis and Landa 1999; Massey and Pyper 2005; Pate et al. 2007; Choorman et al. 2007) (as cited in Chang et al. 2017). Not only is there a decline in the levels of trust, but unionised employees also trust managers less than non-unionised employees (Chang et al. 2017). Demonstrating integrity and trust requires the involvement of unions in the process of engaging employees. Trust is a key element of the psychological contract which can facilitate a new framework for engagement. Employees rely on the union's assessment deciding whether an employer is acting with integrity and if they can trust an employer's motives (Donais 2010; Guest and Conway 2002; Macleod and Clarke 2009; Yarrington et al. 2007).
3. That job design related factors are a critical element of employee engagement (Bailey et al. 2015). Kahn (1990) proposed three main psychological conditions that influence people's engagement and disengagement at work. The dimension of psychological meaningfulness involves a sense of return on investment of the self in work role performance (Kahn 1990). Individuals who experience meaningfulness felt worthwhile, useful and valuable (Kahn 1990). Psychological meaningfulness is highly influenced by the task characteristics of a person's job and these task characteristics that promote meaningfulness are tasks that are challenging, clearly defined, varied, autonomous, challenging, role fit, and involve feedback, opportunities for development, reward and recognition (Kahn 1990).
4. The prospects of delivering engaged employees are significantly influenced by a set of complex internal and external realities unions face, which management must navigate (Donais 2010; Hyman 1975; Jenkins and Delbridge 2013; Salamon 1998). Engagement

needs to be understood in the context of a changing work environment affected by issues such as globalisation, economic downturn, technological advancement and organisational restructuring (Anstey 1997b; Chang et al. 2017). These changes have led to the erosion of union power and enabled organisations to drive increased efficiency and productivity, which is often a trade-off with employee welfare resulting in adversarial employee attitudes towards organisations (Sapelli and Halevi 2009) (as cited in Chang et al. 2017).

5. That employers should see the organisation as a collaborative partnership between all interest groups. A sincere partnership with unions and employees will have a positive influence on engagement efforts compared to the traditional adversarial relationship between parties. (Arrowsmith and Parker 2013; Stewart and Danford 2008; Townsend et al. 2014). Attempts to engage employees without the involvement of the unions will lead to scepticism about the real motives behind any engagement attempts and unions might actively oppose any engagement efforts if employers circumvent them and engage directly with union members (Donais 2010).
6. That it is paramount that employers understand that the success of any engagement strategy requires an adequate understanding of the trade unions' role, as collective organisation in the employment relationship. Unions have various and often competing functions in society, which may lead to unpredictable decision-making on issues of interest to the employers. Involving elected union representatives in engagement efforts is likely to improve as they devote a great deal of time communicating with their members and access to this network is beneficial for employers seeking to engage employees (Donais 2010; Yarrington et al. 2007). The unions can play a significant role in the process feedback mechanisms as they are ideally situated to relay their members' readiness to adopt engagement efforts (Donais 2010).
7. Employers must recognise that unions have the power to influence engagement efforts and that unionised employees place a high value on "voice" in their workplace, a key component of engagement. Communication gives employees a voice which is a key component of any engagement efforts and that engagement can be

enhanced when employees' views are sought through their representatives on strategic and policy matters (Donais 2010; Dundon et al. 2004; Guest and Conway 2002; MacLeod and Clarke 2009; Purcell 2014a; Rees et al. 2013; Yarrington et al. 2007).

8. That engagement must form a key part of the entire EOR by embedding it into the total HRM value chain. The EOR shapes the extent to which people engage with engagement activities. HRM practices which are focused on the three psychological conditions of safety, meaningfulness and availability can directly facilitate and improve employee engagement. This then provides HRM practitioners with the opportunity to combine performance-orientated and employee-orientated HRM practices in their pursuit of engagement (Albrecht et al. 2015; Alfes et al. 2013; Kahn and Heaphy 2014)
9. That leadership and line managers must create a transparent and explicit organisational culture in which unions are empowered to understand the strategic narrative and how they contribute to engagement efforts. Engagement initiatives often rely on line managers' direct involvement with teams and their sentiments towards employees and unions. The literature indicates that transformational leaders bring about a feeling of identification and passion with one's work, which may then have positive effects on engagement (Christian et al. 2011). The quality of LMX also positively affects members' positive emotions and attitudes (Christian et al. 2011). According to Crawford et al. (2014), high-quality LMX promotes psychological safety because it represents a supportive and trusting relationship, which enables employees to perform their daily tasks without fear of negative consequences to their career or selves. Transformational leadership and LMX is not only a significant basis of engagement, but also related to the levels of engagement (Alfes et al. 2013; Arrowsmith and Parker 2013; Donais 2010; MacLeod and Clarke 2009; Townsend et al. 2014; Yarrington et al. 2007).
10. That engagement is positively associated with enhanced individual and organisational performance outcomes. The enhanced individual performance outcome indicators referred to are job satisfaction, organisational commitment, in-role and extra-role performance, life satisfaction and general health (Bailey et al. 2015; Yalabik et al. 2013; Christian et al. 2011; Rich et al. 2010; Macey and Schneider

2008; Holbeche and Springett 2003; Harter et al. 2002), whilst enhanced organisational performance outcomes indicators are customer satisfaction, turnover intention, safety, productivity and profitability (Gupta and Sharma 2016; Harter et al. 2002; Macey et al. 2009; Salanova et al. 2005; Xanthopoulou et al. 2009).

11. That the conceptual framework provides conceptual clarification on employee engagement in a unionised environment to address the low levels of engagement amongst unionised employees as a basis to positively influence competitive advantage. The premise of the engagement framework is that job design factors, individual characteristics, trust and integrity, collaborative partnership, employee voice, HRM practices, and leadership and line manager behaviour are linked to engagement through the three psychological conditions (Kahn 1990), which in turn influence individual and performance related outcomes.

Framework of Engagement

After systematically analysing the literature on engagement, 11 propositions emerged from the evidence synthesis which has been used to create the conceptual framework on how to increase the engagement levels of employees in a unionised environment.

This framework stays true to Kahn's (1990) original work to place the conditions that have the greatest potential to raise the engagement levels in a unionised environment into the conceptual framework. The framework employs Kahn's (1990) theory on the psychological conditions of engagement to explain how individual and organisational antecedent factors can be linked to engagement through the psychological conditions of meaningfulness, safety and availability. Engagement in this framework is a mediating variable between the antecedents, the psychological conditions and engagement outcomes. The framework illustrates how the antecedents extracted from the propositions influence engagement levels and engagement, in turn, leads to positive individual and organisational outcomes.

The framework in Fig. 6.1 illustrates how job design factors, trust and integrity, individual characteristics, collaborative partnerships, employee voice, human resources management practices, leadership and line managers' behaviour influence and individuals psychological experience of work, which in turn drives work behaviour (Kahn 1990).

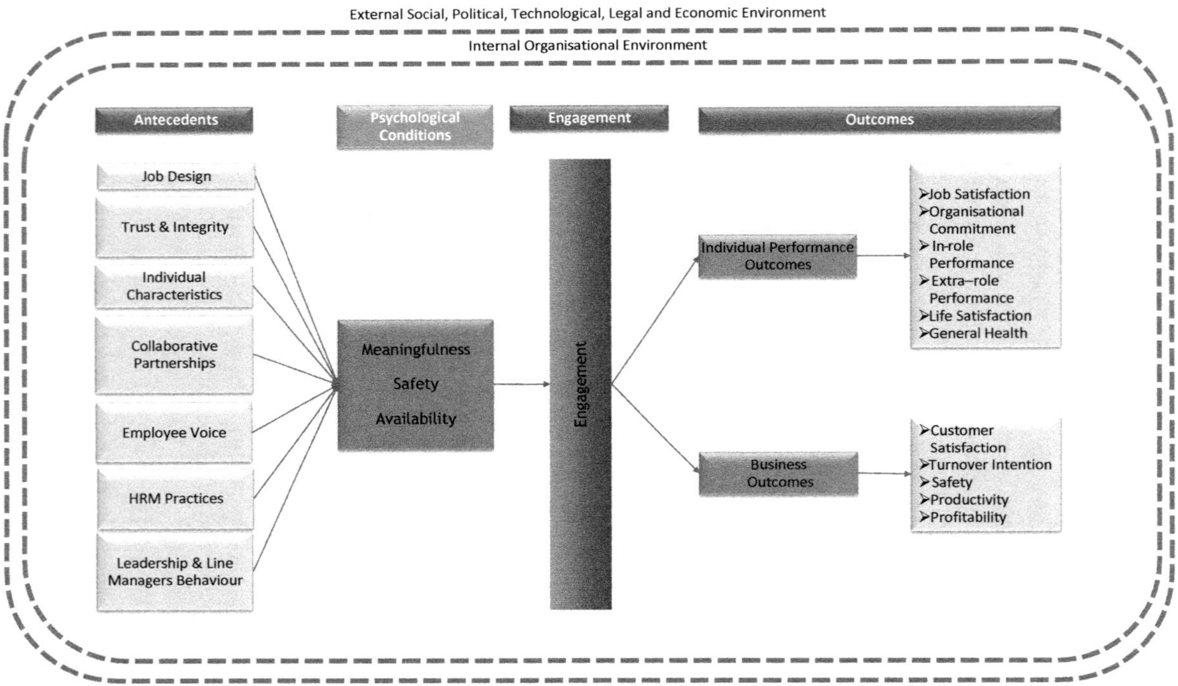

Fig. 6.1 Framework of engagement in a unionised environment

References

Albrecht, S. L., Bakker, A. B., Gruman, J. A., Macey, W. A., & Saks, A. M. (2015). Employee engagement, human resources management practices and competitive advantage: An integrated approach. Journal of Organisational Effectiveness: People and Performance, 2(1), 7–35.

Alfes, K., Truss, C., Soane, E. C., Rees, C., & Gatenby, M. (2013, November–December). The relationship between line manager behavior, perceived HRM practices, and individual performance: Examining the mediating role of engagement. Human Resources Management, 52(6), 839–859.

Anstey, M. (1997a). Employee Participation and workplace forums. Kenwyn: Juta & Co, Ltd.

Anstey, M. (1997b). Labour Relations in Transition: A changing South Africa in a changing world. Port Elizabeth: Mark Anstey.

Arrowsmith, J., & Parker, J. (2013). The meaning of 'employee engagement' for the values and roles of the HRM function. The international journal of Human Resource management, 24(14), 2692–2717.

Bailey, C., Madden, A., Alfes, K., & Fletcher, L. (2015). The meaning, antecedents and outcomes of employee engagement: A narrative synthesis. International Journal of Management Reviews, 00, 1–23. doi:https://doi.org/10.1111/ijmr.12077

Briner, R., & Denyer, D. (2012). Systematic review and evidence synthesis as a practice and scholarship tool. In D. Rousseau (Ed.), The Oxford Handbook of Evidence-Based Management (pp. 112–119). Oxford: Oxford University Press.

Chang, J., Travaglione, A., & O'Neill, G. (2017). Job attitudes between unionised and non-unionised employees. International Journal of Organisational Analysis, 25(4), 647–661.

Christian, M. S., Garza, A. S., & Slaughter, J. E. (2011). Work engagement: A qualitative review and test of its relations with task and contextual performance. Personnel Psychology, 64, 89–136.

Coyle-Shapiro, J. A.-M., & Shore, L. (2007). The employee-organisational relationship: Where do we go from here? Human Resource Management Review, 17, 166–179.

Crawford, E. R., Rich, B. L., Buckman, B., & Bergeron, J. (2014). The antecedents and drivers of employee engagement. In C. Truss, R. Delbridge, K. Alfes, A. Shantz, & E. Soane, Employee engagement in theory and practice (pp. 57–81). New York: Routledge.

Donais, Blaine. (2010). Engaging unionised employees: Employee morale and productivity. Ontario, Canada: Thomson Reuters.

Dundon, T., Wilkinson, A., Marchington, M., & Ackers, P. (2004). The meanings and purpose of employee voice. The International Journal of Human Resource Management, 15(6), 1149–1170.

Eldor, L., & Vigoda-Gadot, E. (2016). The nature of employee engagement: Rethinking the employee-organization relationship. The International Journal of Human Resource Management, 1–27.

Finnemore, M. (2009). Introduction to labour relations in South Africa (Tenth Edition ed.). Durban: LexisNexis.

George, J. M. (2011). The wider context, costs and benefits of work engagement. European Journal of Work and Organizational Psychology, 20(1), 53–59.

Guest, D. E., & Conway, N. (2002). Pressure at work and the psychological contract. London: CIPD.

Gupta, N., & Sharma, V. (2016). Exploring employee engagement – A way to better business performance. Global Business Review, 17(3S), 45S–63S.

Halbesleben, J. R. (2011). The consequences of engagement: The good, the bad, and the ugly. European journal of work and organizational psychology, 20(1), 68–73.

Hall, R. (2015, March 22). Psychological contracts: An introduction to the concept. Retrieved from TAFE NSW: http://www.google.co.za/url?sa=t&rct=j&q=&esrc=s&source=web&cd=1&cad=rja&uact=8&ved=2ahUKEwiQp-zYyOzcAhXpK8AKHRfLCtIQFjAAegQIABAC&url=http%3A%2F%2Flrrpublic.cli.det.nsw.edu.au%2FlrrSecure%2FSites%2FWeb%2F13289%2Fezine%2Fyear_2008%2Fsep%2Fdocuments%2FPsychological-contracts-introduction.doc&usg=AOvVaw0oO4EIZuPHsMSQ0QmdkfLo

Harter, J. K., Schmidt, F. L., & Hayes, T. L. (2002). Business-unit-level relationship between employee satisfaction, employee engagement, and business outcomes: A meta-analysis. Journal of Applied Psychology, 87(2), 268–279.

Holbeche, L., & Springett, N. (2003). In Search of Meaning in the Workplace. Horsham: Roffey Park.

Hyman, R. (1975). Industrial Relations: A Marxist introduction. London: The Macmillan Press Ltd.

Hyman, R. (1987). Strategy or structure? Capital, labour and control. Work, employment and Society, 1, 25–55.

Jenkins, S., & Delbridge, R. (2013). Context matters: examining 'soft' and 'hard' approaches to employee engagement in two workplaces. The International Journal of Human Resource Management, 24(14), 2670–2691.

Kahn, W. A. (1990). Psychological conditions of personal engagement and disengagement at work. Academy of Management Journal, 33(4), 692–724.

Kahn, W. A., & Heaphy, E. D. (2014). Relational context of personal engagement at work. In C. Truss, R. Delbridge, K. Alfes, A. Shantz, & E. Soane, Employee engagement in theory and practice (pp. 83–96). London: Routledge.

Linde, B. J. (2007). Employment Relations, the psychological contract and work wellness in the Higher Education Sector in South Africa. Ridderkerk, Netherlands: Ridderprint B.V.

Macey, W. H., Schneider, B., Barbera, K. M., & Young, S. A. (2009). Employee Engagement: Tools for Analysis, Practice, and Competitive Advantage (First Edition ed.). Chichester West Sussex: Wiley-Blackwell.

Macey, W., & Schneider, B. (2008). The Meaning of Employee Engagement. Industrial and Organizational Psychology, 3–30.

MacLeod, D., & Clarke, N. (2009). Engaging for success: Enhancing performance through employee engagement. Department for Business, Innovation and Skills. London: A report to Government.

Maslach, C., Schaufeli, W. B., & Leiter, M. P. (2001). Job burnout. Annual Review of Psychology, 52, 397–422.

May, D. R., Gilson, R. L., & Harter, L. M. (2004). The psychological conditions of meaningfulness, safety and availability and the engagement of the human spirit at work. Journal of Occupational Organisational Psychology, 77, 11–37.

Nel, P., Kirsten, M., Swanepoel, B., Erasmus, B., & Jordaan, B. (2016). South African employment relations: Theory and practice (Eight edition ed.). Pretoria: Van Schaik.

Purcell, J. (2014a). Employee voice and engagement. In C. Truss, R. Delbridge, K. Alfes, A. Shantz, & E. Soane, Employee engagement in theory and practice (pp. 236–249). London: Routledge.

Purcell, J. (2014b). Provocation series paper: Disengaging from engagement. Human Resources Management Journal, 24(3), 241–254.

Rees, C., Alfes, K., & Gatenby, M. (2013). Employee voice and engagement: Connections and consequences. International Journal of Human Resource Management, 24(14), 2780–2798.

Rich, B. L., Lepine, J. A., & Crawford, E. R. (2010). Job engagement: Antecedents and effects on job performance. Academy of Management Journal, 53(3), 614–635.

Robinson, D., Perryman, S., & Hayday, S. (2004). The drivers of employee engagement. Institute of employment studies. Brighton: Institute of employment studies.

Saks, A. M. (2006). Antecedents and consequences of employee engagement. Journal of Managerial Psychology, 21(7), 600–619.

Saks, A. M., & Gruman, J. A. (2014). What do we really know about employee engagement. Human Resources Development Quarterly, 25(2), 155–182.

Salamon, M. (1998). Industrial Relations: Theory and practice (3rd ed.). Hertfordshire, United Kingdom: Prentice Hall.

Salanova, M., Agut, S., & Peiró, J. M. (2005) Linking Organizational Resources and Work Engagement to Employee Performance and Customer Loyalty: The Mediation of Service Climate. Journal of Applied Psychology, 90 (6), 1217–1227.

Schaufeli, W. (2013). Employee Engagement in Theory and Practice (C. Truss, K. Alfes, R. Delbridge, A. Shantz, & E. Soane, Eds.). London: Routledge.

Schaufeli, W. B., & Bakker, A. B. (2004). Job demands, job resources, and their relationship with burnout and engagement: a multi-sample study. Journal of Organizational Behavior, 25 (3), 293–315.

Sheridan, K., & Anderson, K. (2013, July 24). HR Solutions eNews. Retrieved July 24, 2013, from http://avatarsolutions.com/resources/enews-0311/Unionized-0311.html

Shore, L. M., Tetrick, L. E., Taylor, M. S., Coyle-Shapiro, J., Liden, R. C., McLean Parks, J., & Van Dyne, L. (2004). The employee-organisation relationship: A timely concept in a period of transition (J. Martocchio, & G. Ferris, Eds.). Research in Personnel and Human Resources Management, 291–370.

Shuck, B., & Wollard, K. (2010). Employee engagement and HRD: A seminal review of the foundations. Human Resources Development Review, 9(1), 89–110.

Soane, E., Truss, K., Alfes, K., Shantz, A., Rees, C., & Gatenby, M. (2012). Development and application of a new measure of employee engagement: the ISA engagement scale. Human resource development international, 15(5), 529–547.

Stewart, P., & Danford, A. (2008). Editorial: Union Strategies and Worker Engagement with New Forms of Work and Employment. New Technology, Work and Employment, 23(3), 146–150.

Stumpf, A. S., Tymon, G. W., & van Dam, H. N. (2013, May). Felt and behavioural engagement in workgroups of professionals. Journal of vocational behavior, 255–264.

Townsend, K., Wilkinson, A., & Burgess, J. (2014). Routes to partial success: collaborative employment relations and employee engagement. The International Journal of Human Resources Management, 25(6), 915–930.

Truss, C., Shantz, A., Soane, E., Alfes, K., & Delbridge, R. (2013). Employee engagement, organisational performance and individual well-being: Exploring the evidence, developing the theory. The International Journal of Human Resources Management, 24(14), 2657–2669.

Tsui, A. S., Pearce, J. L., Porter, L. W., & Hite, J. P. (1995). Choice of Employee-Organisation Relationship: Influence of External and Internal Organizational Factors. Research in Personnel and Human Resource Management, 13, 117–151.

Tyler, J. (2009). Employee Engagement and Labour Relations. Retrieved May 31, 2013, from businessjournal.gallup.com: http://businessjournal.gallup.com

Wassel, C. (2013). www.hrsolutionsinc.com. Retrieved May 31, 2013, from HR Solutions, Inc.

Welbourne, T. M., & Schlachter, S. (2014). Engaged in what? Virginia: The Incentive Research Foundation.

Wollard, K. K., & Shuck, B. (2011). Antecedents to Employee Engagement: A structured review of the literature. Advances in Developing Human Resources, 13(4), 429–446.

Wood, G., & Coetzee, J. K. (2006). Negotiated revolutions or evolutionary regime transitions? The Czech Republic, South Africa and Chile. African Sociological Review, 10(1), 234–243.

Xanthopoulou, D., Bakker, A., Demerouti, E., & Schaufeli, W. (2009). Work engagement and financial returns: A diary study on the role o f job and personal resources. Journal of Occupational and Organizational Psychology (82), 183–200.

Yalabik, Z. Y., Potaitoon, P., Chowne, J. A., & Rayton, B. A. (2013). Work engagement as a mediator between employee attitudes and outcomes. International Journal of Human Resource Management (24), 2799–2823.

Yarrington, L., Townsend, K., & Brown, K. (2007). Models of Engagement: Union Management Relations for the 21st Century. AIRAANZ Conference 7–9 February 2007, University of Auckland New Zealand. Auckland: Queensland University of Technology.

CHAPTER 7

Discussion and Conclusion

Abstract This chapter discusses and concludes the findings of the systematic review and narrative synthesis of the literature to address the low levels of engagement in a unionised environment. This chapter concludes that the replacement of the traditional adversarial approach with new management strategies has the most potential of raising engagement levels in a unionised context. The biggest challenge for organisations is to achieve sustainable employee engagement in a unionised environment due to the different expectations unionised and non-unionised employees have from employers. Our framework contributes to the engagement theory and practice in that it is the first conceptual framework to illustrate how antecedents, specifically applicable to a unionised environment, can foster and enhance employee engagement levels in a unionised environment.

Keywords Conclusions • Contribution • Discussion • Raising engagement levels • Traditional adversarial approach

Discussion

The purpose of this systematic review of the literature on engagement focussed on the identification of antecedents that might have the greatest potential to increase the engagement levels in a unionised environment.

J. H. Nel, B. Linde, *The Art of Engaging Unionised Employees*,
https://doi.org/10.1007/978-981-13-2197-9_7

The evidence was synthesised in order to narrate the findings from the various studies to develop a conceptual framework for engagement in a unionised environment.

Various engagement frameworks have been developed since Kahn's (1990) conceptualised engagement illustrating how engagement develops in the individual in response to certain antecedents (Bailey et al. 2015). However, despite the development of these various frameworks, no unique framework for engaging employees in a unionised environment exists. Kahn (1990) still provides the strongest theoretical rationale for understanding the psychology of engagement, as Kahn (1990) is clear about the psychological conditions that are necessary to create high levels of engagement.

Literature reveals that there is a strong body of research indicating that by managing antecedents of engagement, organisations can manage the outcomes of engagement, which in turn have a positive impact on the business outcomes. Despite extensive studies on engagement, there remains uncertainty about what increases levels of engagement. Studies, thus far, offer insight into the experiences of employees with efforts to introduce programmes aimed at fostering and raising levels of engagement in general (Bailey et al. 2015).

The synthesis revealed that the EOR is the main relationship in the labour relations system describing the entire relationship between the employee and the organisation. According to Eldor and Vigoda-Gadot (2016), there is a link between the engagement construct and EOR in that employee engagement is one of the key mechanisms to explain the relationship between employees and organisations and that the EOR in a unionised environment is influenced by a variety of circumstances. The unions' response to these circumstances influences organisations' choice of EOR, and in turn how they increase engagement levels (Tsui et al. 1995).

Evidence showed that unionised employees are less engaged and less satisfied with their jobs than their non-union counterparts (Chang et al. 2017; Tyler 2009). It is clear from the literature that there are significant differences between union and non-union employees and that engaging unionised employees presents different challenges to engaging non-unionised employees. The unique nature of a union's relationship with its members offers advantages to employers seeking to engage unionised employees as unions care about the welfare of their members. If they believe that the engagement effort has tangible benefits for their members, they will be strong advocates for the programme (Chang et al. 2017; Donais 2010). Elected union structures at enterprise level provide an opportunity for ordinary union members to participate in engagement efforts. This offers ordinary union members the opportunity to take part in decisions regarding their job and their workplace (Gollan and Xu 2015; Knudsen et al. 2011).

The traditional adversarial approach founded on the organisations' need to reduce costs, improve profitability, the erosion of union power and the unions' role of protecting job security and the earnings of its members can result in an antagonistic employee attitude towards organisations (Chang et al. 2014). These factors all combine to make engagement efforts more challenging.

The synthesis revealed several prevailing antecedents and additional antecedents are identified, which have the potential to raise engagement levels in a unionised environment. The antecedents and consequences are organised in a conceptual framework that has the potential to increase engagement levels in organisations with a union presence. Engagement in this synthesis examined as a mediating variable in which antecedents influenced engagement levels, and engagement, in turn, leads to individual and organisational outcomes. After examining the most often discussed antecedents and outcomes, 11 propositions on how to increase the engagement levels in a unionised environment were selected to inform the engagement framework.

The replacement of the traditional adversarial approach with new management strategies, such as forging a collaborative partnership with the union, voice, integrity, trust, pluralistic HRM practices, leadership and line manager's behaviour, individual characteristics and job design factors have the most potential of raising engagement levels in a unionised context. It is, however, clear that engagement needs to be considered within a wider political, socio-economic and organisational context (Jenkins and Delbridge 2013).

Many organisations with a trade union presence appreciate the importance of aligning their industrial relations with engagement strategies. In the past, trade unions have expressed wariness about employee engagement, regardless of its potential to provide an alternative participation model (Wright 2011). Successful organisations have moved beyond the old doctrine of strategy, structure, and systems to a softer model constructed on the development of purpose, process and people (de Silva 2013).

Contribution to Engagement Theory

Literature reveals that unionised employees are less engaged than non-unionised employees which, gives impetus for organisations to understand the conditions that will increase the engagement levels of unionised employees. Unhappy workers are also more likely to join unions, although they perceive less LMX consultations, health and safety dispensability, time flexibility, managerial trust, fair treatment and pay equity (Chang et al. 2017). This is especially important as union employees in a unionised environment have the ability to transfer their unhappiness to the entire workforce. Ignoring the low levels of engagement amongst unionised employees is no longer an option for organisations due to the pressure on them to become more competitive. The biggest challenge for organisations is to achieve sustainable employee engagement in a unionised environment, as change is more difficult to bring about due to the different expectations unionised and non-unionised have from employers. It is in light of this reality that a framework was developed to address the lower levels of engagement in a unionised environment.

Through the systematic review of the literature and the synthesis of the literature our study contributes to the engagement theory and practice in the following ways:

1. We developed the first theoretical framework to address the low levels of engagement in a unionised environment.
2. This is the first systematic review and narrative synthesis of the literature to identify specific antecedents that can increase the engagement levels of employees in a unionised environment.
3. Extending Kahn's (1990) framework to create a framework to increase engagement levels in a unionised environment.
4. Identifying additional antecedents to already identified antecedents that have the potential to increase the engagement levels in a unionised environment.
5. Our framework illustrates how antecedents specifically applicable to a unionised environment can foster and enhance employee engagement levels.
6. Identifying that unionised employees are less engaged than non-unionised employees and also experience less job satisfaction.
7. Identifying that although employees join unions in search of more job satisfaction, they never reach the same engagement levels than non-unionised employees.

8. Our findings revealed that engaging unionised employees is different from engaging non-unionised employees.
9. That the long history of adversarialism and mistrust between organisations and union members makes the implementation of engagement efforts more difficult in a unionised environment.
10. Union choices and behaviour impact on non-union members in a unionised environment.
11. Identifying that an engaged workforce does not automatically exist and that organisations must deliberately manage various antecedents to increase engagement levels.
12. Leaders and managers play a vital role in the success of engagement efforts.
13. Change is more successful in unionised environments where there is union involvement in engagement efforts.
14. Implementing initiatives to increase engagement levels are context specific and engagement frameworks must be adapted to the specific environment and the needs of the organisation.
15. Trade unions can influence the outcomes of engagement efforts and that unions are still the most effective way of engaging their members.
16. A new psychological contract with employees must be developed focussing on pluralistic HRM practices.
17. Understanding the skills and competencies needed by leaders and managers to drive high engagement levels.
18. The contribution of propositions that can be empirically tested.

Conclusion

Increasing the engagement levels of employees in a unionised environment is critical, because unionised employees have a considerable ability to influence the entire organisation through collective bargaining. They also have the ability to project their unhappiness to non-unionised employees (Yarrington et al. 2007).

In this synthesis, evidence was accumulated regarding the prevailing antecedents, the additional antecedents and the outcomes of engagement to develop a conceptual framework that can increase the engagement levels of employees in a unionised environment. This is the first narrative synthesis to have considered the body of evidence relating to engagement in a unionised environment with the aim of developing a conceptual framework.

The synthesis revealed that, although it is commonly accepted that union members are not as engaged as their non-unionised counterparts, there are no studies which examine the factors associated with high engagement levels in a unionised environment.

It is, however, possible for union members to reach the same engagement levels as their counterparts (Donais 2010). The synthesis revealed a number of prevailing antecedents and discovered additional antecedents, which have the potential to drive high engagement levels amongst union members. Through synthesising the evidence, a conceptual framework was developed, illustrating which antecedents influence higher engagement levels and may lead to individual and organisational outcomes. Flowing from the synthesis several propositions are selected, which have the potential to increase the engagement levels in a unionised environment.

The synthesis highlighted that no one framework fits all antecedents and different organisations would create engagement in different ways, using different organisational specific strategies and methods (Wollard and Shuck 2011). Saks (2006) in his study on "Antecedents and Consequences of Employee Engagement" also observed that a one-size-fits-all approach to employee engagement might not be viable. Using a matrix of engagement predictors, organisations will better manage engagement and ultimately foster positive business outcomes (Lockwood 2007). Guest (2014b) highlights the need for a viable and integrated approach to employee engagement consisting of practices that may help to enhance engagement, supported by strong evidence-based research.

The presented framework will be helpful in assisting both human resources practitioners and organisations to embrace employee engagement as a strategy to drive high engagement levels in organisations with a union presence.

References

Bailey, C., Madden, A., Alfes, K., & Fletcher, L. (2015). The meaning, antecedents and outcomes of employee engagement: A narrative synthesis. International Journal of Management Reviews, 00, 1–23. doi:https://doi.org/10.1111/ijmr.12077

Chang, J., Travaglione, A., & O'Neill, G. (2017). Job attitudes between unionised and non-unionised employees. International Journal of Organisational Analysis, 25(4), 647–661.

de Silva, S. R. (2013). Elements of a sound industrial relations system. International Labour Organisation, East Asia Multidisciplinary Advisory Team. Bangkok: Bureau of employers activities (ACT/EMP).

Donais, Blaine. (2010). Engaging unionised employees: Employee morale and productivity. Ontario, Canada: Thomson Reuters.

Eldor, L., & Vigoda-Gadot, E. (2016). The nature of employee engagement: Rethinking the employee-organization relationship. The International Journal of Human Resource Management, 1–27.

Gollan, P. J., & Xu, J. (2015). Re-engagement with the employee participation debate: beyond the case of contested and captured terrain. Work, employment and society, 29(2), 1–13.

Guest, D. (2014a). Employee engagement: A sceptical analysis. Journal of Organizational Effectiveness: People and Performance, 1(2), 141–156.

Guest, D. E. (2014b). Employee engagement: Fashionable fad or long-term fixture? In C. Truss, R. Delbridge, K. Alfes, A. Shantz, & E. Soane, Employee engagement in theory and practice (pp. 221–235). London: Routledge.

Jenkins, S., & Delbridge, R. (2013). Context matters: examining 'soft' and 'hard' approaches to employee engagement in two workplaces. The International Journal of Human Resource Management, 24(14), 2670–2691.

Kahn, W. A. (1990). Psychological conditions of personal engagement and disengagement at work. Academy of Management Journal, 33(4), 692–724.

Knudsen, H., Busck, O., & Lind, J. (2011). Work environment quality: The role of workplace participation and democracy. Work Employment and Society, 25(3), 379–396.

Lockwood, N. R. (2007). Leveraging Employee Engagement for Competitive Advantage: HR's Strategic Role. Society for Human Resources Management, 1–11.

Saks, A. M. (2006). Antecedents and consequences of employee engagement. Journal of Managerial Psychology, 21(7), 600–619.

Tsui, A. S., Pearce, J. L., Porter, L. W., & Hite, J. P. (1995). Choice of Employee-Organisation Relationship: Influence of External and Internal Organizational Factors. Research in Personnel and Human Resource Management, 13, 117–151.

Tyler, J. (2009). Employee Engagement and Labour Relations. Retrieved May 31, 2013, from businessjournal.gallup.com: http://businessjournal.gallup.com

Wollard, K. K., & Shuck, B. (2011). Antecedents to Employee Engagement: A structured review of the literature. Advances in Developing Human Resources, 13(4), 429–446.

Wright, C. F. (2011). What role for trade unions in future workplace relations? ACAS. London: ACAS. Retrieved from http://www.acas.org.uk/policydiscussion

Yarrington, L., Townsend, K., & Brown, K. (2007). Models of Engagement: Union Management Relations for the 21st Century. AIRAANZ Conference 7–9 February 2007, University of Auckland New Zealand. Auckland: Queensland University of Technology.

References

Albrecht, S. L., Bakker, A. B., Gruman, J. A., Macey, W. A., & Saks, A. M. (2015). Employee engagement, human resources management practices and competitive advantage: An integrated approach. Journal of Organisational Effectiveness: People and Performance, 2(1), 7–35.

Alcover, C.-M., Rico, R., Turnley, W. H., & Bolino, M. C. (2016). Understanding the changing nature of psychological contracts in 21st century organisations: A multiple-foci exchange relationships approach and proposed framework. Organizational Psychological Review, 1–32.

Alfes, K., Truss, C., Soane, E. C., Rees, C., & Gatenby, M. (2013, November–December). The relationship between line manager behavior, perceived HRM practices, and individual performance: Examining the mediating role of engagement. Human Resources Management, 52(6), 839–859.

Anstey, M. (1997a). Employee Participation and workplace forums. Kenwyn: Juta & Co, Ltd.

Anstey, M. (1997b). Labour Relations in Transition: A changing South Africa in a changing world. Port Elizabeth: Mark Anstey.

Arrowsmith, J., & Parker, J. (2013). The meaning of 'employee engagement' for the values and roles of the HRM function. The international journal of Human Resource management, 24(14), 2692–2717.

Bailey, C., Madden, A., Alfes, K., & Fletcher, L. (2015). The meaning, antecedents and outcomes of employee engagement: A narrative synthesis. International Journal of Management Reviews, 00, 1–23. doi:https://doi.org/10.1111/ijmr.12077

Bakker, A. B., & Demerouti, E. (2007). The Job Demands-Resources model: stat of the art. Journal of Managerial Psychology, 22(3), 309–328.

J. H. Nel, B. Linde, *The Art of Engaging Unionised Employees*,
https://doi.org/10.1007/978-981-13-2197-9

Bakker, A. B., Demerouti, E., & Lieke, L. (2012). Work engagement, performance, and active learning: The role of conscientiousness. *Journal of Vocational Behavior*, 80(2), 555–564.

Bates, S. (2004). Getting engaged. *HR Magazine*

Bendix, S. (2015). Labour relations: A southern African perspective (Sixth edition ed.). Cape Town: Juta.

Bersin, J. (2015). Becoming irresistible: A new model for employee engagement. Deloitte.

Bhuvanaiah, T., & Raya, R. (2014, October–December). Employee engagement: Key to organisational success. SCMS Journal of Indian Management, 61–71.

Bledow, R., Schmitt, A., Frese, M., & Kuhnel, J. (2011). The affective shift model of work engagement. American Psychological Association, 96(6), 1246–1257.

Briner, R., & Denyer, D. (2012). Systematic review and evidence synthesis as a practice and scholarship tool. In D. Rousseau (Ed.), The Oxford Handbook of Evidence-Based Management (pp. 112–119). Oxford: Oxford University Press.

Buhlungu, S., & Tshoaedi, M. (2012). Cosatu's Contested Legacy (First ed.). Cape Town: HSRC Press.

Cartwright, S., & Holmes, N. (2006). The meaning of work: The challenge of regaining employee engagement and reducing cynicism. Human resources management review, 16, 199–208. doi:https://doi.org/10.1016/j.hrmr.2006.03.012

Chang, J., Travaglione, A., & O'Neill, G. (2014). Analyzing job attitudes between unionized and non-unionized. 2014 Cambridge Conference Business & Economics (pp. 1–21). Cambridge: ABER.

Chang, J., Travaglione, A., & O'Neill, G. (2017). Job attitudes between unionised and non-unionised employees. International Journal of Organisational Analysis, 25(4), 647–661.

Christian, M. S., Garza, A. S., & Slaughter, J. E. (2011). Work engagement: A qualitative review and test of its relations with task and contextual performance. Personnel Psychology, 64, 89–136.

CIPD. (2012). Managing employee relations in difficult times. London: Chartered Institute of Personnel and Development.

Cole, M. S., Walter, F., Bedeian, A. G., & O'Boyle, B. L. (2012). Job burnout and employee engagement: A meta-analytic examination of construct proliferation. Journal of Management (38), 1550–1581.

Coyle-Shapiro, J. A.-M., & Shore, L. (2007). The employee-organisational relationship: Where do we go from here? Human Resource Management Review, 17, 166–179.

Crabtree, S. (2006, May). Can Managers Engage Unionized Employees? The Gallup Management Journal. Retrieved from http://www.gmj.gallup.com

Crawford, E. R., Rich, B. L., Buckman, B., & Bergeron, J. (2014). The antecedents and drivers of employee engagement. In C. Truss, R. Delbridge, K. Alfes, A. Shantz, & E. Soane, Employee engagement in theory and practice (pp. 57–81). New York: Routledge.

Cressey, P. (1995, March). Extended Review: Employee Participation. Work, Employment & Society, 9(1), 187–190.

Czarnowsky, M. (2008). Learning's role in employee engagement: An ASTD research Study. Alexandria, VA: American Society for Training & Development.

de Silva, S. R. (2013). Elements of a sound industrial relations system. International Labour Organisation, East Asia Multidisciplinary Advisory Team. Bangkok: Bureau of employers activities (ACT/EMP).

Delbridge, R., & Keenoy, T. (2010). Beyond managerialism? The International Journal of Human Resource Management, 21(6), 799–817.

Denyer, D., & Transfield, D. (2009). Producing a systematic review (D. Buchanan, & A. Bryman, Eds.). London: Sage.

Dhivya, A. S., & Sripirabaa, B. (2015). The impact of leader member exchange on work engagement: an empirical study. International Journal of Management, 6(1), 139–150.

Donais, Blaine. (2010). Engaging unionised employees: Employee morale and productivity. Ontario, Canada: Thomson Reuters.

Dromey, J. (2014). MacLeod and Clarke's concept of employee engagement: An analysis based on the workplace employment relations study. Acas. London: Acas.

Dundon, T., Wilkinson, A., Marchington, M., & Ackers, P. (2004). The meanings and purpose of employee voice. The International Journal of Human Resource Management, 15(6), 1149–1170.

Dunlop, J. T. (1958). Industrial Relations System. Carbondale, Illinois: Southern Illinois University Press.

Eldor, L., & Vigoda-Gadot, E. (2016). The nature of employee engagement: Rethinking the employee-organization relationship. The International Journal of Human Resource Management, 1–27.

Finnemore, M. (2009). Introduction to labour relations in South Africa (Tenth Edition ed.). Durban: LexisNexis.

Fletcher, L., & Robinson, D. (2014). Measuring and understanding employee engagement. In C. Truss, R. Delbridge, K. Alfes, A. Shantz, & E. Soane, Employee engagement in theory and practice (pp. 273–289). New York: Routledge.

Gallup. (2013). State of the American Workplace: Employee engagement insights for U.S. business leaders. Washington: Gallup, Inc.

Gatenby, M., Rees, C., Soane, E., & Truss, C. (2009). Employee engagement in context. Chartered Institute of Personnel and Development, Kingston University, Kingston-upon-Thames, UK.

George, J. M. (2011). The wider context, costs and benefits of work engagement. European Journal of Work and Organizational Psychology, 20(1), 53–59.
Goffman, E. (1959). The presentation of self in everyday life (1st ed.). New York: Doubleday.
Gollan, P. J., & Xu, J. (2015). Re-engagement with the employee participation debate: beyond the case of contested and captured terrain. Work, employment and society, 29(2), 1–13.
Grant, C., & Osanloo, A. (2014). Understanding, selecting, and integrating a theoretical framework in dissertation research: Creating the blueprint for your "house". Administrative Issues Journal, Connecting Education, Practice, and Research, 4(2), 12–25.
Guest, D. (2014a). Employee engagement: A sceptical analysis. Journal of Organizational Effectiveness: People and Performance, 1(2), 141–156.
Guest, D. E. (2011). Human resource management and performance: Still searching for some answers. Human Resource Management Journal, 21(1), 3–13.
Guest, D. E. (2014b). Employee engagement: Fashionable fad or long-term fixture? In C. Truss, R. Delbridge, K. Alfes, A. Shantz, & E. Soane, Employee engagement in theory and practice (pp. 221–235). London: Routledge.
Guest, D. E., & Conway, N. (2002). Pressure at work and the psychological contract. London: CIPD.
Guest, D., & Conway, N. (2003). Exploring the paradox of union worker dissatisfaction. King's College, University of London, Human resource management and employment relations. London: King's College, University of London.
Gupta, N., & Sharma, V. (2016). Exploring employee engagement – A way to better business performance. Global Business Review, 17(3S), 45S–63S.
Halbesleben, J. R. (2011). The consequences of engagement: The good, the bad, and the ugly. European journal of work and organizational psychology, 20(1), 68–73.
Hall, R. (2015, March 22). Psychological contracts: An introduction to the concept. Retrieved from TAFE NSW: http://www.google.co.za/url?sa=t&rct=j&q=&esrc=s&source=web&cd=1&cad=rja&uact=8&ved=2ahUKEwiQp-zYyOzcAhXpK8AKHRfLCtIQFjAAegQIABAC&url=http%3A%2F%2Flrrpublic.cli.det.nsw.edu.au%2FlrrSecure%2FSites%2FWeb%2F13289%2Fezine%2Fyear_2008%2Fsep%2Fdocuments%2FPsychological-contracts-introduction.doc&usg=AOvVaw0oO4EIZuPHsMSQ0QmdkfLo
Harter, J. K., Schmidt, F. L., & Hayes, T. L. (2002). Business-unit-level relationship between employee satisfaction, employee engagement, and business outcomes: A meta-analysis. Journal of Applied Psychology, 87(2), 268–279.
Hirschsohn, P. (2011). The "hollowing-out" of trade union democracy in Cosatu? Members, shop stewards and the South African Communist Party. Law Democracy & Development, 15, 279–310.
Holbeche, L., & Springett, N. (2003). In Search of Meaning in the Workplace. Horsham: Roffey Park.

Hyman, R. (1987). Strategy or structure? Capital, labour and control. Work, employment and Society, 1, 25–55.

Jenkins, S., & Delbridge, R. (2013). Context matters: examining 'soft' and 'hard' approaches to employee engagement in two workplaces. The International Journal of Human Resource Management, 24(14), 2670–2691.

Kahn, W. A. (1990). Psychological conditions of personal engagement and disengagement at work. Academy of Management Journal, 33(4), 692–724.

Kahn, W. A., & Heaphy, E. D. (2014). Relational context of personal engagement at work. In C. Truss, R. Delbridge, K. Alfes, A. Shantz, & E. Soane, Employee engagement in theory and practice (pp. 83–96). London: Routledge.

Kirkman, B. L., Lowe, K. B., & Young, D. P. (1999). High-performance work organizations: definitions, practices, and an annotated bibliography. Greensboro, North Carolina: CCL Press.

Knudsen, H., Busck, O., & Lind, J. (2011). Work environment quality: The role of workplace participation and democracy. Work Employment and Society, 25(3), 379–396.

Konrad, A. M. (2006a, March/April). Ivey business journal. Retrieved from http://iveybusinessjournal.com/publication/engaging-employees-through-high-involvement-work-practices/

Konrad, A. M. (2006b, January 30). The Workplace. Retrieved June 9, 2014, from Ivey Business Journal: improving the practice of management: http://iveybusinessjournal.com/publication/engaging-employees-through-high-involvement-work-practices/

Kular, S., Gatenby, M., Rees, C., Soane, E., & Truss, K. (2008). Employee Engagement: A Literature Review. Surrey: Kingston University.

Kumar, P., & Swetha, G. (2011). A prognostic examination of employee engagement from its historical roots. International Journal of Trade, Economics and Finance, 2(3), 232.

Lawler, E. E. (2001). Designing high performance organisations. Columbia: University of Southern California. Retrieved from http://unpan1.un.org/intradoc/groups/public/documents/un/unpan001316~1.pdf

Leat, M. (2008). Employee Relations. Edinburgh Business School Heriot-Watt University. Edinburgh, Great Britain: Edinburgh Business School.

Lammerts, L., Van Dongen, J. M., Schaafsma, F. G., Van Mechelen, W., & Anema, J. R. (2017). A participatory supportive return to work program for workers without an employment contract, sick-listed due to a common mental disorder: An economic evaluation alongside a randomized controlled trial. BMC public health, 17(1), 162.

Linde, B. (2015). The value of wellness in the workplace: A perspective of the employee-organisation relationship in the South African labour market. Springer.

Linde, B., Schalk, R., & Linde, H. (2008). Clarity and trust: The experience of workplace regulations by employees. South African Journal of Labour Relations, 32(2), 86–103.

Lockwood, N. R. (2007). Leveraging Employee Engagement for Competitive Advantage: HR's Strategic Role. Society for Human Resources Management, 1–11.

Macey, W. H., Schneider, B., Barbera, K. M., & Young, S. A. (2009). Employee Engagement: Tools for Analysis, Practice, and Competitive Advantage (First Edition ed.). Chichester West Sussex: Wiley-Blackwell.

Macey, W., & Schneider, B. (2008). The Meaning of Employee Engagement. Industrial and Organizational Psychology, 3–30.

MacLeod, D., & Clarke, N. (2009). Engaging for success: Enhancing performance through employee engagement. Department for Business, Innovation and Skills. London: A report to Government.

Maslach, C., & Leiter, M. P. 1997. The truth about burnout. San Francisco, CA: Jossey-Bass.

Maslach, C., Schaufeli, W. B., & Leiter, M. P. (2001). Job burnout. Annual Review of Psychology, 52, 397–422.

May, D. R., Gilson, R. L., & Harter, L. M. (2004). The psychological conditions of meaningfulness, safety and availability and the engagement of the human spirit at work. Journal of Occupational Organisational Psychology, 77, 11–37.

Nel, J. H. (1999). An evaluation of the implementation of a Japanese program for workplace improvement in a South African dairy company. Port Elizabeth: Unpublished Master's degree treatise.

Nel, P., Kirsten, M., Swanepoel, B., Erasmus, B., & Jordaan, B. (2016). South African employment relations: Theory and practice (Eight edition ed.). Pretoria: Van Schaik.

Popay, J., Roberts, H., Sowden, A., Petticrew, M., Arai, L., Rodgers, M., … Duffy, S. (2006). Guidance on the Conduct of Narrative Synthesis in Systematic Reviews: Final Report. Swindon: ESRC Research Methods Programme.

Purcell, J. (2014a). Employee voice and engagement. In C. Truss, R. Delbridge, K. Alfes, A. Shantz, & E. Soane, Employee engagement in theory and practice (pp. 236–249). London: Routledge.

Purcell, J. (2014b). Provocation series paper: Disengaging from engagement. Human Resources Management Journal, 24(3), 241–254.

Rees, C., Alfes, K., & Gatenby, M. (2013). Employee voice and engagement: Connections and consequences. International Journal of Human Resource Management, 24(14), 2780–2798.

Rich, B. L., Lepine, J. A., & Crawford, E. R. (2010). Job engagement: Antecedents and effects on job performance. Academy of Management Journal, 53(3), 614–635.

Rigg, J. (2013). Worthwhile Concept or Old Wine? A Review of Employee Engagement and Related Constructs. American Journal of Business and Management, 2(1), 31–36. doi: https://doi.org/10.11634/216796061302229

Robertson-Smith, G., & Markwick, C. (2009). Employee Engagement: A review of current thinking. University of Sussex. Brighton: Institute for Employment Studies.

Robinson, D., Perryman, S., & Hayday, S. (2004). The drivers of employee engagement. Institute of employment studies. Brighton: Institute of employment studies.

Rothbard, N. P. (2001). Enriching or Depleting? The Dynamics of Engagement in Work and Family Roles. Administrative Science Quarterly, 46 (4), 655–684. https://doi.org/10.2307/3094827

Rousseau, D. M. (1995). Psychological Contracts in Organisations: Understanding Written and Unwritten Agreements. London: Sage Publications.

Saks, A. M. (2006). Antecedents and consequences of employee engagement. Journal of Managerial Psychology, 21(7), 600–619.

Saks, A. M., & Gruman, J. A. (2014). What do we really know about employee engagement. Human Resources Development Quarterly, 25(2), 155–182.

Salamon, M. (1987). Industrial Relations: Theory and Practice. London: Prentice Hall.

Salamon, M. (1998). Industrial Relations: Theory and practice (3rd ed.). Hertfordshire, United Kingdom: Prentice Hall.

Scarlett, K. (2013, July 30). Scarlett Surveys International. Retrieved July 30, 2013, from http://www.scarlettsurveys.com

Schaufeli, W. B., Salanova, M., Gonzalez-Roma, V., & Bakker, A. B. (2002). The measurement of engagement and burnout: A two sample confirmatory factor analytic approach. Journal of Happiness Studies, 3, 71–92.

Schaufeli, W. B., & Bakker, A. B. (2004). Job demands, job resources, and their relationship with burnout and engagement: A multi-sample study. Journal of Organizational Behavior, 25, 293–437. https://doi.org/10.1002/job.248

Schaufeli, W.B. (2013). What is engagement? In C. Truss, K. Alfes, R. Delbridge, A. Shantz, & E. Soane (Eds.), Employee Engagement in Theory and Practice. London: Routledge.

Schaufeli, W., & Salanova, M. (2011). Work engagement: On how to better catch a slippery concept. European journal of work and organizational psychology, 20(1), 39–46.

Seligman, M. E., & Csikszentmihalyi, M. (2000, January). Positive psychology an introduction. American Psychologist, 55(1), 5–14.

Shanmugan, A., & Krishnaveni. (2012). Employee Engagement: An Introspection. International Journal of Social Science & Interdisciplinary Research, 1(9), 186–195.

Sheridan, K., & Anderson, K. (2013, July 24). HR Solutions eNews. Retrieved July 24, 2013, from http://avatarsolutions.com/resources/enews-0311/Unionized-0311.html

Shore, L. M., Tetrick, L. E., Taylor, M. S., Coyle-Shapiro, J., Liden, R. C., McLean Parks, J., & Van Dyne, L. (2004). The employee-organisation relationship: A timely concept in a period of transition (J. Martocchio, & G. Ferris, Eds.). Research in Personnel and Human Resources Management, 291–370.

Shuck, B. (2011, June). Integrative literature review: Four emerging perspectives of employee engagement: An integrative literature review. Human Resources Development Review, 10(3), 304–328. Retrieved from http://hrd.sagepub.com/content/10/3/304

Shuck, B., & Wollard, K. (2010). Employee engagement and HRD: A seminal review of the foundations. Human Resources Development Review, 9(1), 89–110.

Shuck, B., Rocco, T. S., & Reio, T. G. (2011). Employee Engagement: an examination of antecedent and outcome variables. Human Resources Development International, 14(4), 428–446.

Shuck, M. B., & Wollard, K. K. (2009). A historical perspective of employee engagement: An emerging definition. In M. S. Plakhotnic, S. M. Nielsen, & D. M. Pane (Ed.), Proceedings of the Eighth Annual College of Education & GSN Research Conference (pp. 133–139). Miami: Florida International University. Retrieved from http://coeweb.fiu.edu/research_conference

Sisson, K. (2008, April). Putting the record straight: Industrial relations and the employment relationship (T. Colling, Ed.). Warwick papers in industrial relations(88), 1–57.

Slabbert, J. A., & Swanepoel, B. J. (2002). Introduction to Employee – Relations Management A Global Perspective (Second Edition ed.). Durban: LexisNexis.

Soane, E., Truss, K., Alfes, K., Shantz, A., Rees, C., & Gatenby, M. (2012). Development and application of a new measure of employee engagement: the ISA engagement scale. Human resource development international, 15(5), 529–547.

Stewart, P., & Danford, A. (2008). Editorial: Union Strategies and Worker Engagement with New Forms of Work and Employment. New Technology, Work and Employment, 23(3), 146–150.

Stumpf, A. S., Tymon, G. W., & van Dam, H. N. (2013, May). Felt and behavioural engagement in workgroups of professionals. Journal of vocational behavior, 255–264.

Townsend, K., Wilkinson, A., & Burgess, J. (2014). Routes to partial success: collaborative employment relations and employee engagement. The International Journal of Human Resources Management, 25(6), 915–930.

Truss, C., Shantz, A., Soane, E., Alfes, K., & Delbridge, R. (2013). Employee engagement, organisational performance and individual well-being: Exploring the evidence, developing the theory. The International Journal of Human Resources Management, 24(14), 2657–2669.

Truss, K. (2014). The future of research in employee engagement. In D. Robinson & J. Gifford (Eds.), The future of engagement thought piece collection, engage for success peer-reviewed thought leadership series. Institute for employment studies. Brighton: Institute for employment studies.

Tsui, A. S., Pearce, J. L., Porter, L. W., & Hite, J. P. (1995). Choice of Employee-Organisation Relationship: Influence of External and Internal Organizational Factors. Research in Personnel and Human Resource Management, 13, 117–151.

Tyler, J. (2009). Employee Engagement and Labour Relations. Retrieved May 31, 2013, from businessjournal.gallup.com: http://businessjournal.gallup.com

Vance, R. J. (2006). Employee engagement and commitment: A guide to understanding, measuring, and increasing engagement in your organization. Alexandria, VA: The SHRM Foundation.

van der Smissen, S., Schalk, R., & Freese, C. (2013). Contemporary psychological contracts: How both employer and employee are changing the employment relationship. Management review, 24(4), 309–327.

Wassel, C. (2013). www.hrsolutionsinc.com. Retrieved May 31, 2013, from HR Solutions, Inc.

Webster, E. (2015). The shifting boundaries of industrial relations: Insights from South Africa. International Labour Review, 154(1), 27–36.

Webster, E. C. (1998). The politics of economic reform: Trade unions and democratization in South Africa. Journal of Contemporary African Studies, 16(1), 39–64.

Webster, E., & Buhlungu, S. (2004). Between Marginalisation & Revitalisation? The State of Trade Unionism in South Africa. Review of African Political Economy, 31(100), 229–245.

Webster, E., & Von Holdt, K. (2005). Beyond the Apartheid Workplace: Studies in Transition. Scottsville: University of KwaZulu-Natal Press.

Welbourne, T. M., & Schlachter, S. (2014). Engaged in what? Virginia: The Incentive Research Foundation.

Whittington, J., Meskelis, S., Asare, E., & Beldona, S. (2017). Enhancing Employee Engagement: An Evidence-Based Approach. Cham, Switzerland: Palgrave Macmillan.

Wickens, P. D. (1995). The Ascendant Organisation. London: Macmillan Press.

Wilkinson, A., Gollan, P. J., Marchington, M., & Lewin, D. (2010). Conceptualizing employee participation in organisations. In A. Wilkinson, P. J. Gollan, M. Marchington, D. Lewin, A. Wilkinson, P. J. Gollan, M. Marchington, & D. Lewin (Eds.), The Oxford Handbook of Participation in Organisations (pp. 3–25). Oxford: Oxford University Press.

Wollard, K. K., & Shuck, B. (2011). Antecedents to Employee Engagement: A structured review of the literature. Advances in Developing Human Resources, 13(4), 429–446.

Wood, G., & Coetzee, J. K. (2006). Negotiated revolutions or evolutionary regime transitions? The Czech Republic, South Africa and Chile. African Sociological Review, 10(1), 234–243.

Wright, C. F. (2011). What role for trade unions in future workplace relations? ACAS. London: ACAS. Retrieved from http://www.acas.org.uk/policydiscussion

Xanthopoulou, D., Bakker, A., Demerouti, E., & Schaufeli, W. (2009). Work engagement and financial returns: A diary study on the role o f job and personal resources. Journal of Occupational and Organizational Psychology (82), 183–200.

Yalabik, Z. Y., Potaitoon, P., Chowne, J. A., & Rayton, B. A. (2013). Work engagement as a mediator between employee attitudes and outcomes. International Journal of Human Resource Management (24), 2799–2823.

Yarrington, L., Townsend, K., & Brown, K. (2007). Models of Engagement: Union Management Relations for the 21st Century. AIRAANZ Conference 7–9 February 2007, University of Auckland New Zealand. Auckland: Queensland University of Technology.

Youssef-Morgan, C. M., & Bockorny, K. M. (2014). Engagement in the context of positive psychology. In C. Truss, R. Delbridge, K. Alfes, A. Shantz, & E. Soane, Employee engagement in theory and practice (pp. 37–56). New York: Routledge.

Index

J. H. Nel, B. Linde, *The Art of Engaging Unionised Employees*,
https://doi.org/10.1007/978-981-13-2197-9

N

O

P

R

S

T

U

V

W

Printed by Printforce, the Netherlands